W9-BZD-162

*"Just look at the grounds left in the empty cup
as if they were clouds in the sky."*

— Sophia's grandfather

It's Grounds for a Good Time

Learn an ancient method of fortunetelling that's ideally suited to today's espresso-charged world.

- Read a fortune in just minutes

- Add a psychic charge to your brew through your preparation ritual

- Increase the effectiveness of your reading by visualizing your questions

- Use the placement of symbols in the cup to learn about the past, present, and future

- Learn the meanings of the most common symbols, from "acorn" to "zodiac"

So take a break from the daily grind and open *Fortune in a Coffee Cup*. It's grounds for a good time.

About the Author

Sophia is a professional psychic and spiritual teacher who has been leading seminars for more than a dozen years, both in Japan and in the United States. From the age of three she was taught fortunetelling by her grandparents. Later she trained further and traveled all over the world, working as a fortuneteller, a teacher, and a professional photographer. The wife of writer Denny Sargent, she provided many of the photos illustrating his book *Global Ritualism* (Llewellyn 1994). She is the author of *Fortunetelling with Playing Cards*, and *Sophia's Fortunetelling Kit*, both published by Llewellyn in 1996. Her website is:

www.psychicsophia.com

To Write to the Author

If you wish to contact the author or would like more information about this book, please write to:

Sophia
℅ Llewellyn Worldwide
P.O. Box 64383, Dept. K610–6
St. Paul, MN 55164–0383, U.S.A.

Please enclose a self-addressed stamped envelope for reply, or $1.00 to cover costs. If outside U.S.A., enclose international postal reply coupon.

For Llewellyn's free full-color catalog, write to *New Worlds* at the above address, or call 1–800–THE MOON.

FORTUNE IN A COFFEE CUP

Divination with Coffee Grounds

SOPHIA

1999
Llewellyn Publications
St. Paul, Minnesota, U.S.A. 55164-0383

Fortune in a Coffee Cup © 1999 by Sophia. All rights reserved. No part of this book may be used or reproduced in any manner whatsoever, including Internet usage, without written permission from Llewellyn Publications, except in the case of brief quotations embodied in critical articles or reviews.

FIRST EDITION
Second Printing, 1999

Cover design by Anne Marie Garrison
Cover art by Eris Klein
Editing by Connie Hill
Interior design by Becky Zins, Anne Marie Garrison,
    Lynne Menturweck, and Connie Hill

Library of Congress Cataloging-in-Publication Data
Sophia, 1955–
      Fortune in a coffee cup / Sophia. — 1st ed.
      p.   cm.
    ISBN 1–56718–610–6 (trade paper)
    1. Fortune-telling by coffee grounds. I. Title.
    BF1881.S66   1999
    133.3'244—dc21   99-19463
                                              CIP

Llewellyn Worldwide does not participate in, endorse, or have any authority or responsibility concerning private business transactions between our authors and the public.
    All mail addressed to the author is forwarded but the publisher cannot, unless specifically instructed by the author, give out an address or phone number.

Llewellyn Publications
A Division of Llewellyn Worldwide, Ltd.
P. O. Box 64383, Dept. K610–6
St. Paul, Minnesota 55164-0383, U.S.A.

 Printed in the United States of America on recycled paper

This book is dedicated to my sister

Roxanne

a keeper of the coffee secrets

Contents

Introduction: Coffee Ground Readings

Reading coffee grounds has been a favorite method of divination among Middle Eastern and African fortunetellers for more than a thousand years. Similar to reading tea leaves, but with more dramatic and easily interpreted symbols, coffee readings offer a quick and fascinating peek into the future that is ideally suited to today's espresso-charged world. Until now, in order to learn the secrets for turning a cup of coffee into a cup of "know," you either had to be close friends with a neighborhood Gypsy, or have spent your formative years hanging out in Middle Eastern coffee shops. This book is the culmination of a thousand years of oral tradition, and I believe the first time these secrets have appeared in print. With the booming popularity of coffee coast to coast, everything needed to divine the future is readily at hand. All you need is a little ground coffee and a clean cup—and this book, of course. The grounds are already in the coffee, no matter if it's drip, espresso, pressed, or from a stand on the street—every cup holds the secret to the coffee drinker's future. With a little help from this book, anyone can transform a utilitarian piece of porcelain into an easy-to-read crystal ball, interpreting the tell-tale shapes that are left behind when the coffee is gone, and enhance their fortunetelling by preparing a special cup of "Joe"—adding a pinch more grounds to the cup just prior to the reading. Readers will learn how to look for the angels, lightning bolts, pots of gold, and future mates that lurk at the bottom of their morning java.

This book shares an important oral tradition handed down to me by my grandfather, who expressed the hope that it would not die with him. I pass this family tradition on to you gladly! Using the directions and interpretations printed here, anyone can learn to read coffee grounds. So skip that daily horoscope—look instead to the bottom of your cup for today's answers.

1

Coffee Reading, My Grandparents, and Me

Although reading coffee grounds to learn about the present or future sounds like a new gimmick, it really isn't. By "reading," I mean viewing the coffee grounds in a person's cup after they have finished drinking it, and using one's psychic abilities to *see* images and omens in the patterns the leftover grounds make. No one knows how old the practice of reading grounds really is, but a conservative estimate puts its origin around A.D. 1000. The use of coffee itself as a beverage is older and seems to have originated in Ethiopia. From there it was brought to Europe by Arabian traders, and eventually spread around the world. Coffee ground readings themselves probably evolved soon after the medicinal and recreational use of coffee was discovered. What likely happened long ago is that the power of coffee was recognized in the spiritual traditions of the area, and its use for divination quickly became part of these traditions.

Coffee ground readings are still popular in the Middle East, Northern Africa, and in the other countries along the Mediterranean seacoast. Even today you will see people involved in readings on the streets in those places. I have seen fortunetellers plying their trade in the local markets and in coffee shops or outdoor cafes, revealing what the future holds for their clients. The art of giving coffee ground readings is passed down by an oral tradition—I have not been able to locate any books or articles on the subject. The tradition, I've been told by my grandparents, was spread slowly around the world by the Gypsies. From Africa to Europe to America, in a roundabout way, this is how it came to me.

The wonderful, interesting, and accurate art of coffee ground reading was passed on to me in the small city of Aberdeen, Washington, when I was just a toddler. My grandparents, native Northwesterners, were fortunetellers who spent their time giving readings to others, counseling them, and telling them their future. They were very involved, I later discovered, in the spiritualist movement of the 1920s, which is a whole other story. My grandfather was born with a veil or caul, a thin extra skin appearing over the head of a newborn baby. It is said to be the mark of second sight, or psychic ability. If the veil is pulled off from the back, the psychic will be able to see the past and if it is pulled off from the front, the psychic will be able to see the future. My grandfather's veil was pulled off from the front—he was an excellent psychic and could see the future easily, or so people said. He was an experienced and sought-out psychic, and I was told that I inherited my gift from him.

I was not born with a veil, but I do have a widow's peak, which by our tradition indicates the same thing, though a veil indicates a much more intense ability and is a rarer phenomenon. As I grew up, I learned from my family many kinds of divination arts—telling fortunes with playing cards, reading tea leaves, and scrying with crystal balls. Later, I became proficient at direct psychic readings and I also learned how to be a medium. This all started when I was three years old!

Reading coffee grounds was the first method of fortunetelling that I learned, at the same time as I learned how to read letters. Some people learn about local history, some learn cooking, and some learn how to play the piano; my family taught me to read coffee grounds for others. My younger sister and I spent many hours at my grandparents' home learning how to read the grounds. Though my grandmother was also a well-versed psychic, my grandfather was my primary teacher. He told me that he learned to read the grounds from the gypsies when he was a boy, at the turn of the century.

My great-grandfather deserted his family, and my grandfather, along with his other family members, moved out to the country and sometimes picked crops in order to make a living. The family later moved into a run-down home near a Gypsy camp—Gypsies did the same kind of work. My grandfather was outgoing, loving, and very funny. His bedroom window overlooked a meadow were there was a permanent Gypsy camp and their music and laughter put him to sleep at night.

He told us that the most beautiful sound he ever heard was the Gypsy king playing the violin at night around their campfire. My grandfather learned to play the violin from this man, and was likewise very impressed by the psychic talents of these people with whom he made friends. As he became closer to them, the king's mother and an older Gypsy woman in the camp taught him divination.

Of the many types of divination my grandfather learned, his favorite was coffee ground reading. He always said that the main reasons were that coffee just tasted better then anything else and that it was so easy and so accurate. Tea leaf reading, he felt, was not as good, though it was and still is obviously more popular. I tend to agree. Coffee grounds just seem to give better information than the leaves. When talking of this, he would say that if you want to know the past, present, or future, then look into a cup of coffee and you will find the answer.

This is as true today as it was a thousand years ago. Cups of coffee hold a lot of information that is easy to pick up. It is very easy to do, once you get the knack of it.

I asked my grandfather how it worked, and he told me, "Just look at the grounds left in the empty cup as if they were clouds in the sky." When you lie on your back and look at clouds, you can see so many different shapes, and they are always shifting. They can be anything your imagination wants to make them. A cloud could be a house or an apple. It does not matter what it *really* looks like—what you see with your inner eye is what matters. Everything that you see in an empty cup streaked with coffee grounds has a meaning. Everything resembles a symbol, and you must take those symbols, translate them, and weave them into meaning with the help of your inner vision.

What makes readings personal and helps the reader pick up on things is that the people who are about to get a reading carefully drink the coffee first, while thinking about their questions. That makes it *their* coffee and *their* fortune. I was taught that the essence of the person is left in the cup, and the reader must then convey the meaning and practical information left there to the person.

My family would often sit around a stove on typically rainy Northwest days. My sister and I would be given cups of coffee, no bigger than doll cups, to which we would add a pinch of extra grounds to make more interesting readings. My grandfather would drink out of his big white cup and then slowly turn the cup counterclockwise three times, all the time concentrating on what his questions would be or what his desires were. He would then wait for the last of the coffee to drip out. He would finally pick up his cup and begin to read, while we sat fascinated and entranced.

As we asked questions or he explained key points, we would remember them and later apply them to our own little doll-cup readings. He would often coach us or correct us. We loved our coffee cups and they seemed to hold all the mysteries of the universe. My grandfather was not only a very good and kind man, he was also incredibly accurate with his readings and often predicted things no one could have known. Because of his modest fame in our small coastal city, he was a popular person to visit. This began to affect my life as well.

My grandfather once said to me that he was counting on me to learn how to read the grounds and be better then anyone. I took his advice seriously, and when his friends dropped by to have their fortunes read, as they often did, I would be the first person to do it. I was the *warm-up* reader before my grandfather gave them the serious reading, and so I, a little child, would look into their cups to see what their fortunes were. I had a natural talent for this and soon I was being requested for readings. My grandparents treated this art as a very spiritual thing, not as a game. They felt that to be a psychic was a gift from God, and taught me to never take my powers for granted. My grandfather said that, like any such gift, it must be shared and treasured and never forgotten. Never use it lightly, he cautioned me, or for entertainment. As my grandparents got older, they stopped telling fortunes so much. My grandfather said that it was harder for him and made him feel sad to *see* so many things that were problems for others.

Like any activity, the more you do it, the better you get at it, and this was a pleasure for me. I still love to give readings and I feel that I am improving at it.

One day a man came to get his fortune read and my grandmother introduced him to me as: "the man who always had work during the depression." Joe would stop by to see if we needed anything, and he always had something to give us, usually a sack of apples or a loaf of freshly baked bread. My grandparents never asked a fee for readings, it was against their spiritualist beliefs, but everyone knew that you should give something for a reading—it was implied. Usually a form of barter is what happened.

One time, when Joe came, my grandfather said, "Try the granddaughter out, she's learning and she is pretty good at what she does." He would drink the coffee in my grandparents' company and I would go outside to play or walk across the street to see the neighbors' horses until I was called back into the little house to read the grounds. I loved the special attention, but I did not want the responsibility that I was being compelled to shoulder. I guess it was like anything that you are not sure about in the beginning, I looked at these things as mystic chores. Later I learned that it was a service that I could do to help others so they could make decisions about what they needed. Joe was very respectful of me and what I had to say. The difficult part for me as a kid was to sort out fact from fantasy—that is, what it was that I needed to concentrate on. This is still the key skill, to find the best way to look at the psychic picture *as a whole*. It was difficult when I was young because I had to think, "what can I, a kid, say to a grownup that will make sense?"

Joe was a simple man, so I could explain to him what I saw in my own terms and this was okay with him. One day when I was looking in his cup, I saw the number "2" at the top of the cup—that meant two hours, and it was near a $ sign and a bird. I interpreted these simple symbols for him. He would get good news soon that would involve money. Joe thanked me and left. Later that afternoon he called to tell us that he had received a letter with $200 in it. Apparently he had overpaid his taxes and the money was a refund! These kinds of coincidences happened regularly after readings. It wasn't strange to me at all, and no one told me that it was unusual.

As time went by, I became more accurate in my readings and grasped the complexities more completely. I started giving readings to my girlfriends. I liked doing readings when my subject and I had more in common. I was especially good at picking up on their boyfriends' names, and if they had a future together or not. One girlfriend was in love with a man whose initials were L.O. These initials never did appear in her cup, but another man's did—the initials J.D., with a ring next to them. The location of the initials indicated that it was somebody in my friend's future, and the ring meant that it would be a serious relationship. We knew everybody in town and we could not figure out who J.D. could be. He turned out to be an older man outside of our circle of friends and he did marry my friend sometime later. They are still married. The husband does not believe us about this reading, but we love to tease him about it.

Often it seems that details I pick up don't mean anything at the time, but later they turn out to be right on. What you *expect* doesn't matter; what is important is the design of the grounds and what you *see*. I was taught it is necessary to always be honest and tell people what you see. I did then and I continue to do so today. One of my grandparents' greatest desires was that I write down their teachings and share them with the world.

When I was a child, people who became readers had been born with the gift. They usually learned about divination through a relative or as an apprentice. There were no classes or workshops as there are today, and a reader had to prove him- or herself constantly. Our family accepted only donations—we never had a set fee and we never advertised. As in any small town at the time, people were born into a family and continued to work within the family business. Members of our family worked at fortunetelling, boat building, and on cars. Later they were involved in logging, which was not an option for me. Things are different today than when my grandparents were alive.

When you give a serious and successful reading—an easy thing to do once you learn how—people will be amazed and will always be asking for readings. At a wedding recently, I spent several hours upstairs giving readings instead of dancing, but it was fun and my accuracy shocked a lot of skeptical people. It is fairly easy to give coffee ground readings, but you need to learn the basics, and it is difficult to find someone to teach you how to do them unless you travel to the Middle East.

This is what you are looking to accomplish when you are doing a coffee ground reading: finding information that relates to another person and developing the easiest way to get the information across. With a little knowledge, which is provided here, you can go a long way. Anyone can learn to read the grounds—all you need is an empty coffee cup, imagination, and this book. The only other thing you need is an open mind.

When you look at an empty cup, at first all you see are streaks of grounds, but look closer, let your mind open, what else do you see? Perhaps a *ring*? Is someone about to get married? How about that *bird*—are they about to hear some good news? What about that *question mark*—are they questioning somebody or faced with a big decision? After you see the symbols, look up the meanings in chapter 4 of this book (using your intuition as well), and then you will have a fortune to tell. It's that easy!

Practice on your friends and family. Soon you will be good at it, and able to tell a complete stranger their fortune in two minutes. I've done coffee ground readings on television, at special social gatherings, in my office, and in various seminars, but you can do it in your own home (as my grandfather did in his), or in a coffee shop as they do along the blue Mediterranean seacoast. I have simplified many of the teachings I received from my grandparents and distilled them in this book so that anyone can give a clear and informative reading in a short time. So, brew up a delicious cup of coffee, open up this book, and soon you will be on your way!

2

GETTING READY TO READ

From beginning to end, the art of making coffee for fortunetelling is an important ritual. A cup of coffee that is prepared or blessed correctly contains a psychic charge that results in a better reading. Coffee ground readers in Turkey and Egypt always insist on grinding, brewing, serving, and sharing the coffee with their clients before actually reading the grounds for them.

For centuries people have had a sociable cup of coffee together, and then looked for their fortunes in the grounds—much like finding the surprise in the cereal box when you were a child. It is the same with the grounds. What is it that you will find? A long-ago secret? The initials of the new romantic love of your life?

A long-awaited trip? This chapter explores the spiritual side of coffee preparation in a light-hearted way.

Choosing and Preparing the Coffee

Though any type of coffee except instant can be used for fortunetelling, beans that you choose, grind, and prepare yourself will add to the experience and fun of giving coffee-ground readings. The origin of the coffee used for readings can be very important. As people pick and roast the beans, their feelings, thoughts, and psychic impressions fill the coffee beans. How they are grown also influences the beans: Were they grown naturally or mass produced? Were they allowed to ripen naturally or filled with chemicals? I always suggest to people who take coffee ground reading seriously that they begin as serious chefs do—with the best, freshest ingredients. A search for organic coffee picked by people who are treated decently will pay off in the long run. You will begin your reading with a clean slate and you will know that your reading is not tainted with negative feelings or vibrations.

If you don't have control of the coffee, then the next best thing you can do is psychically banish or cleanse the coffee. Hold the beans in your hands and chant:

> *Out, tout, throughout and about*
> *All good come in, all evil go out!*

Visualize all negativity flowing out of the coffee and into the earth. Wash your hands and then begin your coffee preparations.

In this way the water you use should also be as pure as possible. The same chant can be used over the water, if you wish, or you can simply drop a single grain of salt into it and say:

> *Pure as snow, pure as rain,*
> *Pure as the sea, you be again.*

Heating the water to a boil, prepare the clean cup (white is always best) and the coffee. As the water comes to a boil, circle the collected cup, boiling water, and coffee three times with your left hand, clockwise, and say the simple charm that follows.

Force of fire, joy of water
Cup of knowledge, beans of earth
By steam and dream give wisdom birth!

Pour the water into the coffee-maker. As it brews, visualize white light streaming into it. A prayer for wisdom to the deity of one's choice is appropriate now. When it is done, add a pinch of dried grounds directly into the cup and sprinkle a bit onto the ground as thanks to the Earth for this wonderful coffee. You may say:

Thanks to the home, thanks to the hearth
Thanks to the Spirit of Mother Earth.

These are just a few of the simple rituals I have used and that you can use as well. Always adapt them to your own intuitive ideas and beliefs.

First, if there are not enough grounds in the coffee cup when you are getting ready to read them, simply add another pinch of grounds directly to the cup and stir it three times clockwise. You may need to do this with almost every reading to get the right amount of grounds to read easily. In the old days percolators or old coffeepots always left enough grounds in the cup, but today's French presses and other coffee-makers are too efficient! The more grounds, of course, the clearer the images. However, don't add so much to the cup that you can't drink it!

Hint: Let the coffee stand a few minutes; the grounds will settle nicely and not get stuck between your teeth!

The Cup

Any cup or container can be used to read coffee grounds, including the plain paper ones from the local deli, but simple, rounded, white porcelain cups are best because they show the patterns better than others. To make the most out of your reading, the type of cup must be considered. People who are quite serious about coffee ground reading often have one or two cups that they use *only* for reading. It is traditional to keep the cup wrapped in a white cloth when it is not in use.

No matter what cup you use, rinse it quickly with water before using it, and wipe it dry with a clean towel. Visualize all previous energies flowing away, leaving it pure and open for new impressions. How the cup is held, treated, and *charged* are all important to the effectiveness of the reading. A few simple charms and visualizations like this will ensure a great reading. One simple but effective charm is to visualize the cup as the "holy grail," or the cauldron of wisdom. Hold the empty cup up and say:

> *Dome of stars above, dome of earth below*
> *Pour in divine light, all of darkness go*
> *By the chalice of light, may we all grow.*

Anyone intending to give a reading should prepare for the experience a bit, even if is only a reading for yourself! This can be done very easily with a few quick thoughts and gestures. Banishing all unimportant thoughts, focusing intent, and then asking for divine guidance are the three most important steps to follow. All of this can be done internally, very simply, with little outward sign. I often banish mentally by envisioning a circle of white light about me, driving all negativity away. Then I focus my mind and will on the cup as a single point of light. Finally I ask my Guardian Angel to help me help another with truth and love. This is, of course, a very personal thing to do, so it will vary with each reader. I strongly recommend something like this be done to increase the accuracy of the reading.

It is also important for the people receiving the reading to prepare for it. As a reader, I often tell them to close their eyes, banish all distractions from their minds, focus on the "light within," and silently ask for knowledge. Words like these, or something similar, should be said to whoever is receiving the reading. It will help them focus and listen to what you are going to say.

So, the coffee is brewed, a bit of grounds are added to the cup, the coffee is poured (in silence please). The next step is to offer the cup, *handle first,* to the person for whom you are reading. Then they must drink the coffee, or at least part of it, while intently thinking about their question or questions. Have them hold the cup in both hands and really *put themselves into* the cup. When they are ready and after the cup is handled in this way, the excess dregs should then be slowly poured out as the cup is turned by the person being read *three times counterclockwise,* as it is also being turned upside down, so that all excess coffee pours out onto the saucer you have provided. This is very important (see photos, pp. 32–33).

Only then is the cup passed to the reader and the grounds are examined, with careful attention paid to where the grounds have settled.

Mental Preparation

Now, a few words on reading the grounds and the mental state necessary to do so correctly.

It does not take a rocket scientist to read the grounds. What you need to do is focus and concentrate on what you want to understand, but do not push too hard! First, always be clear about why you are doing the reading. Sometimes I don't do a reading for myself after I have gotten a little clarity from pausing to reflect. A little meditation goes a long way. If you are clear about the reading, then take a moment to invoke the divine for some guidance. As I said, I'm partial to my Guardian Angel (or sometimes the Boddhisattva Tara), but whichever way you wish to bring it into your life, spend a moment doing this before the reading—it will help you see truth.

It is also important to keep in mind what it is that you want to know. In reading the grounds do not think of your grocery list, errands that you must run, or other *must dos*. Instead, ask the grounds why you are here reading them, and what it is that you want to see. Interested in money? Then think about money questions. Interested in love? Then think about love questions. Want to know about health? Then think about and clearly visualize your health questions.

It is possible to have a reading on one or as many subjects as you want. If there are many things that you want to know about, you will want what I call a general reading. To see what is news in general, it is best just to enjoy your cup and not think about any particular subjects.

If I am reading the cup for another, then I always ask the person before I begin: "What do you want to learn from this reading? What is it that you want to resolve or to understand when we are finished?" This gives them time to think, and helps them focus as well. Telling someone to focus, but not giving them some advice on how to focus, will give them the cue to relax and to concentrate. This will make for a better reading.

While concentrating when I read the grounds, I am focusing on problems or feelings about which I need a little more understanding before I make a decision on the best course of action. My grandfather used to give the people who came to see him for a reading time to talk and to relax—it was a way to help the energy move into the cup. Have you ever noticed that when you talk or think about a problem or a good idea the objects around you pick it up? If you are angry, sometimes a treasured object will break. If you are about to have a good idea, then you will find that you will have some unusual good luck, with things working out better then planned. This is why it is important to take advantage of the cup. It will help you understand what is happening around you, and it is just plain fun.

Whenever I do a reading for myself, the moment when I know I'll be able to read the cup comes when I begin daydreaming of the days when I backpacked throughout Europe as a young adult. Here is how my "coffee daydream" goes:

Images float into my mind. I remember the white buildings against the blue sky and water on the islands of Greece. In outdoor cafes I would see people giving readings out of one another's cups. The remote island of Crete was a healing place for me, where I went as far as I could until I ran out of land and could not go any further. I was sent here with visions in my dreams—a voice told me I must go to Crete. The smell of the coffee from that island transports me back to the feelings that I had when I was there.

See how I transported my mind? As I enter a state of free-association with my own dreams, I am soon ready to read. Daydreaming creatively is a skill you will develop with coffee-ground reading:. Let your mind drift when reading the cup, let the coffee smell take you away as it does me. It should be the same when you drink your own coffee. It is not necessary to think of Greece, but it is good to concentrate on forgetting your problems and then on *floating* mentally. You will soon see images in the grounds.

The Method

When I read for myself, I first boil the water, as mentioned. I grind the beans in a coffee grinder, and then I prepare a French press coffee maker. I add the grounds and never forget an extra pinch in the cup. I like my coffee dark, so I put a lot of coffee grounds in my French press, add the boiling water, and press the handle down to make the coffee.

Usually the coffee that is made for readings in the Middle East and in Africa is dark and thick. Think of Turkish coffee and you'll get the idea, though my coffee isn't quite that thick!

My favorite cup for readings is one my husband made for me, and it is just the right size. I drink my coffee and think about what type of day is ahead of me. I banish all negative or interfering thoughts and put a circle of light around me. I ponder: Will I have a good day, a busy day, or a day when nothing seems to go right? What is it that I want to know? I drink my coffee and think of these things. If I just want a general reading that day, I drink my coffee without thinking of anything at all. If your house is like my house, your routine might be similar. Many mornings I just drink my coffee and get my family off to work and school. After they leave I finish my coffee, silently ask my Guardian Angel for guidance, and then sit down to read the grounds. I pour out the rest of the coffee that is in the cup, while turning the cup counterclockwise three times as I tip it upside down. The grounds tend to coat the inside and the edge of the cup, and I can then read what they tell me (see photos, pp. 32–33).

Many times what appears in the cup is part of a subject's subconscious. There are three significant zones in the cup: the top or rim, the middle, and the bottom. In the bottom of the cup is the past, or the subconscious. I was reading one woman recently—in the bottom of her cup she had in the grounds the initial "N", and not a whole lot else. That was okay, because she wanted to really understand about "N", the man that she lives with who was the focus, the love of her life, even though she did not think it was the best relationship for herself. She had many questions. The grounds are tools for understanding what it is that we want to know.

1. Adding extra grounds

2. Stirring to blend in grounds

3. Begin pouring

4. Turn counterclockwise

5. Turn and pour

6. Continue to turn and pour

7. Final (third) turn ends with handle down

8. Residue of grounds ready to read.

9. In this cup one can see the images of an elephant, a fish, a snake, and the letter "S".

I have read the grounds from coffee prepared in many types of coffee makers, from percolators to espresso makers. The procedure is always the same; you enjoy your cup of coffee and focus or concentrate on what you want to know. If I am in a coffee shop and I want to read my grounds, I just ask the *barrista* to put a little extra grounds in another coffee cup. After I am almost finished with my cup, I add the grounds, swirl them in and around my cup, then turn the cup upside down and see what is in the grounds. When I do this, I normally have people come up to my table, wanting to be read or to learn how to do it themselves. There are special coffees such as Turkish or Greek that are perfect for readings. I usually have a cup of this in Greek restaurants, and I have met other grounds readers at these restaurants.

The Science of Ground Reading

The coffee grounds hold many secrets and they have the answers. I have been asked how this works—how I can *read* the essence of another person? I believe the answer lies in DNA. We know that when our mouth touches a cup it leaves our own personal evidence—we plant our DNA. The grounds then translate the DNA into symbols such as numbers, letters, and of course images. The DNA is your blueprint, the message that is your destiny. If you unravel your message, then you know what your calling is in life—why you are here.

It is the job of the reader to decode your message—the grounds help by translating from the subconscious into the conscious mind of the reader, telling her or him what you really need to know or understand. What our destiny is in life is always inside of us—our talents, our hopes, and our desires. I believe DNA reflects our destiny or *True Will*. How we get lost in our lives is by listening to what others believe we should do to be happy. For instance, what if you want to be an artist and you have talent, but your family thinks you would be better off doing something more practical, like an office job that will pay the bills? Conflict happens when you know that others want you to live a specific life, but your DNA is telling you something different—it subconsciously holds the pattern to what you should be doing, your real will.

A good reader will find the clues to this in your grounds. The grounds are connected right to the source—the imprint of your mouth, and your inner-most being. Your DNA translates to the images, letters, and numbers of the grounds. If you read the grounds, secrets that have been lost can be found. Good luck and remember: *knowledge is all*.

3

FINDING AND INTERPRETING THE SYMBOLS

A reader looks for any obvious patterns that might be symbolic or filled with meaning. Do this quickly, without pushing yourself too hard. It takes a bit of nurturing—after all, you're only looking at smudges of coffee grounds in a cup! Once you have the knack, it isn't difficult to do at all. In fact, if you find it difficult or wearing, it is a sure sign that you are doing it wrong!

The whole process is like daydreaming. Remember Rorschach inkblot tests? The ones where someone shows you a blot of ink on a piece of folded paper and you are supposed to say what it looks like, or the first thing that comes into your mind? Well, reading grounds is a lot like that. It is an exercise in *active imagination* and requires the same "what do you see?" kind of talent. The idea is to let go and simply let your unconscious mind *find* images in the chaotic patterns of the grounds left in the cup.

Before you attempt to read coffee grounds, try these simple exercises:

1. Go to the ocean shore or a riverbank, stare at the water patterns, and look for images. Don't think too much; just let go of your thoughts. It will be hard at first, but it will become easier.

2. On a sunny day, lie on the grass and look at the clouds. Totally relax. Close your eyes and then open them. What do you see in the clouds? Write it down, if you feel like it. Do this ten times—it will get easier.

3. Take a plate or other flat surface. Mix a little water and dirt together (make it watery), then splash it on the surface. Look quickly. What images do you see? Try to find at least three images. Wash it clean and do it again. Repeat this ten times. When you can do this easily and quickly with no real effort, you're ready to read coffee grounds!

What to Look For

Some really simple patterns have meanings that affect the images when you are reading, so let's start with them first:

- Many clustered specks may indicate movement

- Clear lines show that plans must lead to a specific goal

- Wavy lines show uncertainty

- Poorly outlined things show indecision or obstacles

In addition, numerous key symbols can be found in the grounds. For example: A boat or airplane may indicate a journey. Big coin-like dots mean that money is involved in the situation. Initials can indicate people. Arrows indicate specific answers of "yes" or "no." Angels, apples, cats, bells—all of these and many more symbols or images indicate different things that have happened or that will happen, depending on where they appear in the cup. Use the meanings section, chapter 4,

to help decode the symbols in the grounds, and the cup
diagram here to determine their locations.

- Bottom part of the cup = past

- Middle part of the cup = present

- Top part of the cup = future

- Near the handle of the cup = more intense
  for the person being read

In addition to images in the cup, you will also look for numbers or letters of the alphabet. Numbers often can represent time: if you see a number in the bottom of the cup for instance, like a three, it was something that happened three days or months ago (or it will happen in three hours, days, or months). If you see the number three in the middle of the cup, it means an event is happening that was planned or began three hours, days, or months ago. If the number three is on the rim of the cup, it shows that after three hours, days, or months time a change in a major event will occur. If the number is large it probably means months, if very small it indicates days. For instance, if there is a small number three in the bottom of the cup, then the event took place three days ago. If the three is small and is on the rim of the cup, then it will happen after three days.

It is very unusual to see years indicated in a cup because coffee grounds are normally instant readings. In fact, in all my years of reading the grounds and also in my grandfather's experience, we rarely saw anything that indicated years. If you do get the image of years, the number three will be very large, but faint and ill formed, almost too difficult to read—that indicates years, but the way that I tend to interpret it is that fate could change drastically. If seen in the bottom of the cup, and the number three is so ill formed that it looks like a child drew it, it would indicate that something major happened in your life three years ago that changed it drastically. If seen in the middle of the cup, the number three would show that for three years there has been an influence that now alters events. If the number is seen on the rim of the cup, you would have a major life change in three years.

Letters of the alphabet often represent people, so if you see a letter or letters in a cup, it usually indicates someone's initials. If a letter of the alphabet is on the bottom of the cup, then that person is someone that you have known for many years or someone from the past. If seen in the middle of the cup, it indicates someone who is close to you or someone you think about all the time. If seen on the rim of the cup, it shows a person with that initial(s) will be coming into your life.

A key to understanding the importance of initials and letters in general in readings is seeing what they are near. For example, say you see a plane near the rim of a cup with the initial "M" near it. You might ask the question "Are you flying to see a friend whose name begins with 'M' soon, or are they possibly coming to see you?" Chances are, the person you are reading will be shocked and tell you that one of these two things is true. If you see these images and they are close to the handle, you can be sure that "M" is a lover, a very best friend, a husband/wife, or a relative!

Because the cup is considered the dome of the heavens, the placement of the symbols, as mentioned, is very important. The closer images are to the rim, the closer the events are to the present. If a symbol is at the bottom of the cup, it means that the event is in the past; if at the very center of the bottom, it is in the far-distant past. If the images are seen in the middle of the cup, it is what surrounds you now—the size shows how immediate it is. A very large airplane in the middle of the cup shows an important trip happening *now*, or very soon! The handle is a point of connection between the cup and the person who is holding the cup, and therefore is always a key area to consider in a reading. Anything near the handle of the cup, any type of image at all, is in the area of strength and therefore is a strong image for the person getting the reading—one could even say intense. Numbers, letters of the alphabet, or images tend to be stronger, and more powerful here. Look at it this way—like something you love with a passion—that is the difference between seeing something anywhere else in the cup and here in the *place of strength*.

Chapter 4 contains interpretations of the symbols and images you may find in your coffee grounds. The first sentence or two of each meaning is printed in bold lettering. Use this information for fast, simple readings that are not in-depth—a morning reading in that commuter cup of coffee on the bus, a fast reading for a friend at work, or possibly a quick break-time reading about a specific question for yourself ("How will that report I wrote be accepted?" or "Will I have a weird or great blind date tonight?"), for instance.

The balance of the interpretations for each image is more thorough, giving specifics on how the meaning changes with placement in the cup—the bottom/middle/top interpretations that go into greater depth, and pinpoint the timing you can expect. They also contain a number of my personal observations, examples from my own readings, and a lot of funny stories! You will want to use the entire meaning when you are doing a deep or serious reading for someone. Maybe a woman is having "man trouble," another friend is thinking of quitting a job, or possibly a pal is about to make a major business deal. You need to take these readings a bit more seriously and so you need to be more thorough and concentrate more deeply on what the symbols mean. When doing readings for a fee, I always go into the full meanings in explaining the symbols to a client.

One more note on image meanings: I have listed just about all the meanings handed down to me from my grandfather, but I know that there are many other symbols that may appear in a ground reading. I recently saw a CD in someone's cup—it turned out that they were working on a recording for a major label! A CD is not listed in the meanings section—I saw that and interpreted it myself. This will definitely happen to you as well.

If you find in someone's cup an image that is not listed, just open your mind and give it the meaning you feel is right at the time—don't worry, you'll probably be right! You will want to make a note of it for future use.

The hardest part of reading is after you have cleared your mind, had your friend drink his or her coffee and pour out the dregs, and found the images. Then you have to put it all together into a *story* of sorts—this is the reading. I take time to examine the cup, note all the images and symbols I see, note where they are in the cup, look to see if there are any numbers or letters, and then take a big breath and begin. It is easiest to start at the bottom, the past; work your way up to the present; and then finish with the future, making sure to note if anything is near the handle. I sometimes do it this way, but I've been reading so long now (over thirty years) that I often drift from one part of the cup to another, making connections as I *feel* them. After a while you'll do this as well.

A lot depends on the person you are reading for, so don't be afraid to ask questions: "Do you have a friend with the initials M.P.?" "Are you going to take a trip soon?" "Will you be doing a business deal in the near future?" All of these questions and more are perfectly natural—you'll need some help to interpret the images to fit exactly the life of the person you are reading, so don't be bashful! You are a coffee-ground reader, not a mind reader. Give and take will help you tie all the images together into a reading that explains things for that particular person—the purpose of the whole thing.

Chapter 5 contains a number of sample readings that I taped and transcribed so that you could read what *real* readings sound like. Your readings will, of course, be different. Don't worry, it is an art and everyone's way of doing art is always different! Just be natural and take your time. At first it will be difficult, but soon it will get easier and eventually it will be a snap.

My final advice is to have fun with this! It is not necessary to take coffee-ground reading seriously. I have found it a great way to break the ice, to meet interesting people, and to get people interested in me! It's great fun at parties! I have happily passed the time on car, bus, train and plane trips by giving and getting coffee-ground readings—and it is almost always enjoyable! Unlike other forms of fortune telling, it is not necessary to take this so very seriously—there is nothing wrong with people not believing it! Trust me, after some practice, people will begin to believe you when you start getting things right over and over again—and you will get things right. Anyone can do coffee ground-readings, as long as they have a little imagination, know how to daydream, and are able to focus a bit on others—it is easy!

So, focus yourself, banish the boring everyday world, pour a cup of coffee, open your heart to a little truth, and look in the cup—a whole world is opening up in there, ready for you to interpret and enjoy! Wake up and smell the coffee! Then, read it!

4

MEANINGS OF THE SYMBOLS

What follows are a number of symbols (listed in A–Z sections) that might be seen during a coffee-ground reading. Every possible symbol cannot be listed here. Your imagination may also provide a number of additional symbols; these are equally valid and important. Using your intuition and "inner eye" during coffee ground readings is the most important part of reading. Here then are some of the most common symbols I've encountered and what they mean.

Note: If the specific symbol you see in a cup (example: a ROSE) is not listed here, look under a more general heading (example: FLOWERS)—then alter the interpretation a bit to fit the person you are reading. Just use your intuition.

Acorn

This shows the questioner is a lover of the outdoors;
it may also reveal those with a green thumb

This image appeared in the cup of a client who owned a
nursery. In another client's cup it revealed that he was a
forest ranger. In the bottom of the cup, it shows that
small beginnings lead to greatness. Just as an acorn
grows from the mighty oak, so does an idea. In the middle of the cup, this symbol shows that you make your
best decisions outside—not in your home or office. To
get fresh ideas, go outside and take a walk. When
appearing on the rim, the acorn shows the urge to

spend some time in the great outdoors or on the green (golfers take note).

Airplane

This shows that a trip on an airplane is coming up, or there may be a strong desire to get away from it all

I have seen this image more often in the cups of flight attendants than anywhere else. In one woman's cup I saw an airplane and two initials. Her boyfriend's name started with those initials—he was a pilot. When an airplane appears in the bottom of the cup, it shows that thoughts are firmly planted in the air. If others call you an "air head," then you can blame your cup. When it appears in the middle of your cup, it shows you have a deep love of traveling; you are always planning your next trip. When it appears on the rim of the cup, it shows that either your bags are packed because you are going away on a trip soon, or that you are an armchair traveler.

Alien

Friendship and love! This image is almost always a certain type of person who is unusual or from another part of the world or universe

It shows you attract people who are different from the rest. I saw this symbol in one young man's cup—he told me he was the alien and always felt different from others. "Alienated" is a better word to describe this feeling. In the bottom of the cup, this symbol shows an unusual past or a friendship that is a bit out of the ordinary. When it appears in the middle of the cup, it shows that you are about to have an exotic house guest. When it appears on the rim, it shows that you are about to meet someone who is out of this world.

Alligator or Crocodile

This shows that you should use caution in any speculations or new business ventures

Think about all those teeth and the possibility of them crunching down on you. Watch out for those you think you can trust. Be especially wary if there is an initial next to the symbol, indicating a questionable person. It is easier to slow down than to make a quick decision that may soon spell disaster. When this symbol appears in the bottom of the cup, it shows that you have been cheated out of money in the past. In one woman's cup, it revealed that she felt violated that she did not get her money refunded from a particular business deal. The alligator in the bottom of the cup told her it was not going to happen. In the middle of the cup, it shows that you may be starting a business venture that you could regret later. When it appears on the rim, it shows that you are about to make an unwise business decision.

Almonds

This shows good fortune in the home and at work

This is really a nice image, conjuring up visions of the Middle East where coffee readings began. When it appears in the bottom of the cup, it shows you have a nice family and are well supported in your lifework. When it appears in the middle of the cup, it reveals that you are about to feel much better about your life and the road you have chosen. When it appears on the rim, good fortune is headed your way.

Ambulance

This shows a speedy recovery: you can tell it is an ambulance and not a car if the letter "A" appears on the image

This was on the bottom of one man's cup, indicating that he had a speedy recovery when he was young. He then told me about a near-fatal car accident that he was involved in many years previously. When it appears in the middle of the cup, it shows that you need to take it easy or you could have an accident. When it appears on the rim, it shows that you should watch out for any hidden health problems or accidents now.

Angel

*This brings good news; someone is
watching out for you, and you are well
protected from harm*

This is a wonderful sign of feeling safe wherever you
might go. When it appears in the bottom of the cup, it
shows that you were watched over in childhood. A feeling of being overprotected or smothered might be typical. When it appears in the middle of the cup, it shows
that you are protected from harm. When it appears on
the rim, good news will soon arrive.

Anchor

*If seen clearly and well formed, it's a fortunate
sight, but if the anchor is not that clear and
more out of form it indicates disappointment*

In one cup a person had two anchors, one well-formed
and the other slightly blurred. Since the images were
next to each other, and so was the letter "V," it indicated

a situation where the man could not decide if he was fortunate or disappointed with his lover "V." When I asked him if "V" stood for "Vixen," he laughed and said, "You got that right." When this image appears in the bottom of the cup, hold on tight to what you know is yours—that gut feeling you have will never steer you wrong. When it appears in the middle of the cup, watch for what you want, your desire is headed your way. Your ideas about this may change though, especially if the anchor is not well formed. When it appears on the rim, you are about to convince others of your beliefs, especially if someone has challenged your belief system.

Apple

This is a very fertile time for creativity, great for all artists—there is no such thing as a bad apple in a cup

In the bottom of one woman's cup the apple indicated she had always wanted to be an artist, and she had been very creative since early childhood. When an apple appears in the middle of a cup, it shows active creativity. I saw it in an older man's cup—he made his money as an art manager. When it appears on the rim of the cup, it means success, I found an apple in my cup when my first book was accepted by a publisher. An apple is the symbol for art that is all-consuming.

Arch

Money in business matters and love affairs

No matter where this turns up, you will benefit from another person's generosity. What is more fun than spending someone else's money? It does not show earnings, just a nice little bonus that is difficult to turn down. An arch in the bottom of the cup shows someone from the past or an older relative who will help you with money. When it appears in the middle of the cup, it shows a business deal with a love that may be too great to pass up. When it appears on the rim, look forward to a brilliant opportunity.

Arrow

If the arrow points up, then the answer to a question is yes; if it points sideways, the answer is maybe; if it points down, the answer is no

Arrows are one of the more frequently seen images in a coffee cup. It must be because when someone is about to have their grounds read they always have some sort of question. The arrow is very easy to spot, and has similar meanings in any location, except for timing. When it appears in the bottom of the cup it is the past, in the middle the present, and at the rim the future.

Ax

This shows an act of bravery that mystifies and thrills your friends; you will be a hero due to a courageous act startling all who know you

This symbol was on the rim of a cup I read; it turned out that the man had saved someone from a burning building. He also went in and knocked on every door in the apartment building and yelled for everyone to get out. A humble man, he did not see this as anything anybody else would not have done. As a thank you, a grateful relative who is a client of mine gave him a reward: to have a reading. He chose coffee grounds and I saw an ax in his cup. I told him that he was very brave and a hero, but he was shy about it. So unassuming was this man that he had not told me what he actually did—my client later told me. Not everyone with an ax in their cup is going to save someone from a burning building, but if the ax is there you are a brave person who is no stranger to courage and depth of character. When it appears in the bottom of the cup, it shows that throughout your life you will be called on to aid others and make a difference. When it appears in the middle of the cup, it shows you are a person of strength and make a difference in this world. When it appears on the rim of the cup, be strong; an act of bravery will soon be required.

Baby

*When this symbol appears, expect news
about a bundle of joy soon*

One never knows how a soul wants to enter the world.
When I saw this image in one woman's cup, I told her
to expect news of a baby. She told me that she was too
old for that. I said that it did not have to be for her, it
could be a grandchild or the child of a friend. She
thought she was too young to be a grandmother (at
fifty-five, I sincerely doubted her claims, especially since
she told me later that her son was twenty-five and married). Well, guess who called me later with the news that

a baby was coming into her life? If you do not want a child, then be careful when you see this symbol. You may get a surprise package! When it appears in the bottom of the cup, you are connected with a child from the past who will be contacting you soon. I have seen this in cups of people who have given up a child for adoption, and had the child contact them later in life. When it appears in the middle of the cup, expect to hear news of a baby soon. When it appears on the rim, it means a baby is in your future.

Ball

Moving on to a bigger and better lifestyle, your world is rapidly changing

I saw this symbol in the cup of a woman who was off to graduate school in another country. A ball signifies a change in life: that once-in-a-lifetime chance to make yourself over, a challenge that will open you up to new worlds. If the ball appears in the bottom of the cup, you have not had the ball rolling for some time and you have not moved forward on an old dream. This omen suggests it is a good time to try. If it appears in the middle of the cup, you are about to change your lifestyle and the way you live your life completely. If it appears on the rim of your cup, life will be moving faster than you can keep up with. Whenever the ball appears in the cup, expect change to get the ball rolling.

Balloon

To drift on to another place or to change residences; moving without a lot of direction; a sojourn in life that leads you merrily down the garden path

For those of you who want to drift along in life, this is a fun symbol. If it appears in the bottom of the cup, you must have moved around a lot in life when you were a child or you daydreamed most of the day away. In the middle of the cup, it means you are about to send yourself along some wonderful journey.

When it appears on the rim, restless soul that you are, let go of the string and see where you drift off to. I once saw this in someone's cup. He was a mime who made his living traveling from one European country to another, and I met him in a sidewalk cafe in Paris.

Basket

Someone or something is standing in your way; walk around the basket, don't kick it over

This is really an obstacle—do not try to work it out, some things in life are better if you go around them. A basket symbolizes a time such as this. Look at the image like this: baskets easily tip over and can hold a variety of things. You need to proceed cautiously, not to knock the basket over, spilling out the contents. Go slow. A basket in the bottom of your cup indicates that your past is going to be your future. Be careful not to repeat any mistakes. If the basket appears in the middle of the cup, you are about to upset the status quo. If it appears on the rim of the cup, be careful of making a friend into a foe; remember to walk around the basket—do not kick it, or everything will fall out.

Bat

Longevity; when you see these nocturnal creatures, it is a symbol of friendship as well as a long healthy life

Bats are a good-luck symbol in China. When I have given readings in the Far East, people always ask me if they have a bat in their cup. They know the meaning of the symbol. Also, the bat can mean that many times it is a stranger who comes into your life and helps you. If it appears in the bottom of the cup, you have had the same friends for a long time and it is important for you to remain friends for life. If it appears in the middle of the cup, you will have a long and happy life. If it appears on the rim, a stranger will approach you and offer help.

Bear

A bad mood has left you unbearable; it is time to stop arguing with all those you meet

In a very loud and hostile way, a woman who came to see me kept questioning everything that I said. Of course she had a bear in her cup. It was sad though—she told me that she drove everybody nuts because she always questioned them so much. If it appears in the bottom of your cup, a bear indicates a gruff disposition. If it appears in the middle of the cup, your attitude drives others away, so unless you like being alone you should watch what you say. If it appears on the rim of the cup, watch out for any meanness.

Bed

Beware of misfortune; if you are careful
and think thoroughly before you act
on any decisions, then good fortune is yours

This is not a good sign for the careless; if you act before you think things through, you are on the verge of misfortune. I saw this in my cup when I was a teenager, and it helped me slow down enough to wait until I made a decision and to thoroughly think about what lies ahead instead of just plunging forward, which was my natural tendency. If it appears in the bottom of the cup, you have made some poor long-term decisions. If it appears in the middle of the cup, you are in the middle of making a major decision, but be careful and not over-anxious in your decision making. If it appears on the rim, you will soon learn whether you made the right decision or not.

Beetles

Do not quarrel with your friends;
sometimes untrue gossip
surrounds you

If spied in the bottom of your cup, false friends have influenced you in your past. In one reading I saw this image and discovered the person had been involved in a lawsuit for slander. A former employee had spread many unkind and untrue stories about my client, who then sued the ex-employee for slander. If this symbol appears in the middle of the cup, your neighbors have nothing to do but spread rumors about you. Ignore them. If it appears on the rim of the cup, pick your friends carefully and do not give out private personal information about yourself.

Bells

Good news or marriage is coming your way; if the bell is standing upright, good news; if the bell is ringing you will receive great news

If you are planning to get married, or love to go to weddings, this is really a fortunate sign. My uncle and his bride had this in their cups right before their wedding day—he was eighty-five and she was eighty when they tied the knot. If it appears in the bottom of the cup, it tells of news from the past. If it appears in the middle of the cup, you are surrounded by good fortune. On the rim of the cup it shows you are about to receive some good news.

Belt

Take it easy, do not overdo, especially with eating

I have seen this in many readings of people who were dieters or people concerned with overeating. I have seen this also in people who should be more concerned with their weight. If it appears in the bottom of the cup, you spend a lot of time worrying about food or overdoing it. If it appears in the middle of the cup, take it slow— you are pushing your body too hard. If it appears on the rim of the cup, watch it—you are about to overindulge; Remember, it is near the holidays when we tend to overeat!

Berries

Social activities of a happy nature; berries have the same meaning

If there is more than one berry, then the social function is large. In one neighbor's cup, berries showed up on the rim when she was on her way to a very large family reunion. She was concerned because her husband's family had to drive from five states away with their four children (all under age six). It turned out to be a very pleasant experience for everyone. If this image appears on the bottom of the cup, you have many pleasant memories. If it appears in the middle, you are frequently included in or planning social events. If it appears on the rim, buy some new clothes—you are about to be invited to a wonderful party.

Bicycle

You are on the right path to obtain your goals

If you wonder which direction you should go, don't worry—you are correct. With a single-minded direction you will definitely get to where you are headed. Whatever you do, stay on the path that is ahead of you. If a bicycle appears in the bottom of your cup, remember what it is that you always wanted to do—that is your true path. If it appears in the middle, you are headed in the right direction—pass go and collect your $200! If it appears on the rim, it means that after trying to make up your mind you finally will decide in what direction to head to achieve your goals. Fame and fortune ahead.

Birds

Good news is headed your way, especially for those in sales or self-employed; opportunities for business success are great

Any type of bird, from big to small, is a symbol of good news in business. If you need to learn the results of a business transaction, look in your cup for the answer. If the bird appears on the bottom of the cup, look for the answer yes to come for a long-awaited business deal. If the bird appears in the middle, it signifies great success in anything you undertake now. If the bird appears on the rim, you are about to take off in business in a completely different and wonderful way. Often travel is involved.

Blankets

You are a warm-hearted person, the first to donate at fund raisers and a volunteer who has helped the world a lot in small ways

If a blanket appears in the bottom of your cup, you tend to give until it hurts, but much is returned to you. Give and get, you understand the true order of the world. A pet peeve of yours is selfish people—you have no patience with those who hoard when they have so much. If this image appears in the middle of the cup, you are busy helping others. I have seen this frequently in the cups of social workers. If it appears on the rim, you will spend a lot of time helping others and in turn others will help you. Reward.

Boat

You are going away on a trip, but may find romance is just around the corner; dreams of romantic places for those who want to be swept off their feet

If a boat appears in the bottom of your cup, you are an incurably romantic person who sees the world through rose-colored glasses. If it appears in the middle of the cup, you have had to make a decision—which way should you go in life? Do you drift around or do you sail ahead? If it appears on the rim of the cup, you're about to cross over and sail toward a long-awaited dream.

Bones

An inner strength comes from deep inside of you; strong and steady, you are a person others look up to

If this symbol appears in the bottom of the cup, you have taught yourself at a young age how to be strong and reliable. If it appears in the middle of the cup, you have the strength to do what you need to do in life to be successful. If it appears on the rim of the cup, you are about to be relied on by others to lead. I once saw this symbol in my cup, and later that day was asked to take an important position in my son's school. It was not the type of activity that I like to do, but someone was needed to take this responsibility on, so I did it.

Books

A great time to learn something new; gain a deeper understanding of yourself through reading and listening

It is a time to be quiet and not boastful. Another meaning is that you are a writer or have seriously thought about a book that you always wanted to write. If the book is well formed, then your ideas are very firm on what you want to write about. If the book is not so well formed, then it is difficult to decide what type of book you would want to write. If it appears in the bottom of the cup, it's a mark of intelligence. If it appears in the middle of the cup, you are about to learn or be taught a new lesson. If it appears on the rim of the cup, it's the start of a learning adventure.

Bottle

Your intake of alcohol causes you problems, or you have problems with a friend who drinks too much

This is a warning sign that overindulgence will catch up with you or a loved one. It can give you a lot of insight into what is really going on in someone's life, or it could show, if it appears in the bottom of the cup, that drinking was once a problem. If it appears in the middle of the cup, you are in a party mood—enjoy yourself but don't overdo it. If a bottle appears on the rim, you need to guard against overindulging every weekend, or when you have any other chance to unwind.

Bowl

Prosperity will soon be yours, you are in a position to share

If the bowl is upright, you can be helpful. Through your generosity, your loved ones or community will greatly improve. If the bowl is tipped, then what you gain will soon disappear unless you plan carefully. If it appears on the bottom in the cup, you come from a family of means. If it appears in the middle of the cup, money is headed your way. If it appears on the rim of the cup, you are about to make some very important financial decisions.

Box

A surprise awaits you, maybe a gift from a lover, or you get a special unexpected present

If this symbol is in the bottom of your cup, a surprise that has always been a secret desire will soon be yours. In the middle, it shows the surprise is coming your way soon. On the rim, it means that now is a good time to expect a great surprise. I always get asked the same question when someone gets this symbol in their cup. "Is it a good surprise in the box, or is it something I do not want?" My answer is that it is a wonderful surprise; my grandfather taught me that a box is never a negative symbol.

Bread

You need to nurture yourself or another person, treat yourself kindly, or care for a special pet

Bread is a symbol that you must also take care of your health or the health of something or someone else who depends on you. In the bottom of the cup, it means you must start to nurture your destiny more or poor habits will catch up with you in a way that is not positive. In the middle of the cup, it shows you spend too much time helping others to the point where you are spreading yourself thin. It is okay not to push so hard. On the rim, it shows you are in a position to be of great benefit to others.

Bridge

You are on the verge of making some major decision that will alter your life— which way should you go?

Will you take the bridge that will bring change? It is not an easy choice and the results are final. In one man's cup, I read that he was about to make a decision about moving from his small town to a large city. He had lived his whole life in the small town and was nervous about leaving it all behind—the family business and all that he knew that was familiar, just to try something new. He understood that if he left—crossed the bridge—he would never be able to return to the town he left behind. His role in his community would be changed forever. If a bridge appears in the bottom of the cup, you have made some difficult decisions in your life that not only greatly influenced you, but loved ones as well. In the middle of the cup, it shows a little courage goes a long way when crossing the bridge. If it appears on the rim it shows there are further questions on what to do. Remember, not making a decision is a decision.

Broom

You are getting in shape and cleaning up yourself and your surroundings; a major overhaul of your personal appearance is expected here

Spending a lot of time remaking yourself is prominent. Will you change your home to match your new look? In the bottom of your cup, this image shows that in the past frequently you changed yourself as well as your surroundings. I saw a broom in one woman's cup. She changed herself completely whenever she started a new relationship; it was as if she was in disguise. In the middle of the cup, it shows you are now deciding what kind of look you want for yourself and your home, or you are thinking of moving and changing your lifestyle completely. If it appears on the rim of the cup, prepare for that new look—you are ready to take off.

Bubbles

A sign of gaiety; parties and enjoyment;
the more bubbles you have the better the time

This appeared in the cup of a seventy-five-year young man who was invited to more social events than he could attend—he was fun to be around. I saw this image in the cup of a woman who rarely went out, but she was changing her ways and about to really live. If the bubbles appear in the bottom of the cup, you have had a lot of good times and are an enjoyable person. In the middle of the cup, you have the skills to throw a wonderful party. On the rim, it shows you should get out the dancing shoes: a good time will be had by all.

Bugs

A warning to act cautiously, as there are
unfortunate influences around you

Any creepy crawler (human or otherwise) fits here, except for spiders—they have their own special meaning (see p. 229). If this symbol appears in the bottom of the cup, it shows your subconscious or past is at work. You have hidden much from others—a secret identity perhaps. One man who had a bug symbol in his cup told me that he was under the witness protection program. If it appears in the middle, watch out for creepy hidden or subtle influences. This shows you how the grounds bring up many important characteristics that are causing you problems. If a bug appears on the rim of the cup, watch where you step, you might have a gooey bug underfoot.

Bull

You have an aggressive co-worker who is out to harm you, so stay out of his or her path

This is a great omen because, if you do not know who your angry co-worker is, you are about to find out who is in your way. I once did a group reading for a psychiatric clinic. All the workers had a bull in their cup and everyone knew who I was talking about when I explained the meaning of the bull. A woman they worked with was a mean person whose only delight in life was to destroy others in a petty bureaucratic way. In fact, they all started laughing. They knew she was a past problem and a continuing future problem. In the bottom of the cup, if the bull appears, it shows you have lost out in the past to a meddling co-worker. If it appears in the middle, do not tell this person a thing, keep going on with what you want to do. If it appears on the rim, avoid the bull; it will bring misfortune to attempt to negotiate with her or him.

Bushes

*You have a much more realistic
view of yourself and others*

Insight is a blessing now. Your wisdom is surprising and others look to you as a person with grace and insight, so use your gift wisely and you will benefit many. If it appears in the bottom of the cup, it shows you can use your gift from past experiences to help many others. If it appears in the middle, others look to you for support and strength; your endurance will help others greatly. On the rim, it shows you are about to take a leap of faith and help others with your strength.

Butterfly

A sign of happiness, you feel young and bright; this can also mean a younger person who greatly affects and influences you

In reading for a mother and daughter, I found that both of them had this image inside their cups. They lived together and brought much to their relationship in that they acted more like sisters and best friends than a mother-daughter team. If a butterfly appears in the bottom of the cup, then you are entirely youthful in appearance and/or personality. If it appears in the middle, it's a great time to have the youngest people in your life show you something new. If it appears on the rim, you are about to step off into an adventure that will make you feel youthful.

Cabin

*A cabin shows a romantic idea about your home;
the difference between a cabin and a house is
that the cabin always has a chimney*

It shows possessiveness about your home and belongings that you like to share with loved ones. You enjoy private times in your cabin. If seen in the bottom of the cup, you are spending too much time daydreaming about the perfect home. In one man's cup, it showed that he spent his weekends looking for that perfect cabin getaway. He did find it and he moved his family there to live year-round. If a cabin appears in the middle of the cup, you are about to finally settle comfortably in your own place. If the cabin is seen on the rim, the day-dreams you have had in the past are now ready to become reality. Enjoy!

Cake

Good fortune and fulfillment of desires; how sweet it is—yes, you can have your cake and eat it too!

If you have one desire that is really strong, then it is time for it to be fulfilled. If a cake appears in the bottom of your cup, your secret desire—known to very few—is about to become a reality. If it appears in the middle of the cup, good fortune is here or just around the corner. If it appears on the rim, get plenty of sleep because the world will soon belong to you. Life is to enjoy.

Camel

Difficulties and worries; you are holding yourself back from true happiness

Take a deep breath. Ask yourself what it is that is holding you back from what you want to do in life. Many times it is another person or unlucky situations that place you in unfortunate circumstances. This is not the best time to take on anything new. If the camel is on the bottom of the cup, your past is holding you back from enjoying the present, sometimes from an extensive debt. If it appears in the middle, you are surrounded by difficulties and worries—remember that they will soon pass. If it is on the rim, you are about to suffer from misfortune, but if you plan ahead you will be able to avoid or lessen its effect.

Camera

Someone is watching you; good if you enjoy being in the limelight, but if you like to be left to yourself, then you are in for surprise

If this symbol appears in the bottom of the cup, others notice you—if you are a model or an actor, it's a wonderful symbol. If it appears in the middle of the cup, you are about to have heavy scrutiny, so be on your best behavior at home and work. If it appears on the rim, the spotlight will be on you soon. I once saw this image in a reading for a co-worker who was about to have her class observed.

Candle

This is a good omen for insight, drive, and energy

If it appears in the bottom of the cup, it shows insight into the past—great for historians or antique dealers. It shows you truly understand how everything works.

This symbol appeared in the grounds I was reading for a man who was a rare book collector. If it appears in the middle of the cup, you spend a lot of time processing information, which gives you clarity and insight. If it appears on the rim, you spend a lot of time thinking about the future.

Cane

Beware of all business deals for a couple of days; now is not the best time to make any investment decisions

If the cane has initials next to it, it is unwise to trust anyone with those initials. If it appears in the bottom of the cup, long-time business ventures may prove to not be good investments—wait a while longer. If it appears in the middle of the cup, it shows this is a time when you need to proceed with caution, go home and think about it for a couple of days before making a decision. If it appears on the rim, watch out for any upcoming business that sounds too good to be true. It just may be.

Canoe

**A canoe indicates a lack
of friends; you are
too isolated and lonely**

Spending much time alone is fine if you want to live in a monastery, but if you live in the real world like most of us, it can be a lonely place. If the image of a canoe appears in the bottom of the cup, it suggests being out of touch with reality—you may spend too much time at home or watching television. If it appears in the middle of the cup, you need to find others who share your interests. If it is seen on the rim of the cup, then either a move has you feeling misplaced or you lack friends. When I see this in my cup, I make plans to go out more and enjoy life.

Car

If the car has strong lines a trip is indicated, but if the car has broken lines or is unclear then car trouble is ahead

My grandfather added this symbol when the horse and buggy days were over. Make sure you determine if the image is well formed or ill formed. If it appears in the bottom of the cup, and the car is well formed, it shows a long trip; if it is ill formed then you need to replace your old car. If it appears in the middle of the cup, a fun vacation is happening if it is well formed, or it means car problems if it is ill formed, so check your automobile before hitting the road. If it appears on the rim of the cup, a long trip is coming up if it is well formed, or look out for future expensive car trouble if it is ill formed.

Cards

*Good fortune and money
is coming your way*

Look closely at this to see if you have another symbol in the cup such as clubs, hearts, spades, or diamonds. If it appears on the bottom of the cup, money from the past will catch up with you. If the image includes a club in the bottom, then it is money that you have earned which is due to you. If it is a heart, someone will give you money. If it is a spade, a lawsuit or judgment will be won. If a diamond appears, you could win money. If a card appears in the middle of the cup, fortune and good luck are around the corner. If the card has a club on it then you earned your good luck and fortune, if it is a heart then you'll receive love through friends and family; if it is a spade, then you have waited a long time to have good fortune. If you have a diamond, you have good fortune because of your intellect. If it appears on the rim, expect a great new beginning. If the card appears to be a club, the new beginning will be work-related, if it is a heart, it will be an emotional beginning such as a new relationship, if it is a spade then you have earned a new beginning that is full of adventure. If it is a diamond it means a start with some new capital or some sort of financial gain.

Carpet

You have a very wonderful friend, and you enjoy the better things in life together

This is truly a warm and close relationship. I have spied this image in many cups when two friends have come for a reading together. It appears in the bottom of the cup when you have had a close friendship for many years, just like siblings. If it appears in the middle of the cup, you enjoy the same activities together. If it appears on the rim, you and your friend will have many years of friendship ahead. If you have a carpet in your cup, you are truly blessed with friendship.

Castle

*Isolation and overwork is trying your soul;
it's time to let down the drawbridge*

This is the symbol of an overachiever who has forgotten
how to enjoy him or herself. If spied in the bottom of
the cup, it shows you can achieve any long-term goal
and get the desired effects, if need be. If it appears in the
middle of the cup, you are about to realize that all work
and no play is very unsatisfying and you'll start to enjoy
life more. If it appears on the rim, it shows that after
reaching your work goals you feel a need to reach out to
others and you'll start to bring down the drawbridge.

Cat

*You have a secret and it is best to keep
quiet about what you know right now*

No need to tell the world about your news,
take the attitude of a cat: do not talk and certainly never
come when you are called! If this image appears in the

bottom of your cup, it shows family secrets are starting to surface. If it appears in the middle of the cup, you are wearing a look of total satisfaction because you have the goods on another, but now is not the time to spill the beans. If it appears on the rim, secret knowledge is to your advantage. In a reading for a reporter, it appeared that she was about to break an amazing story. She asked if she should tell some of her friends who were also reporters. The cat in her cup told her the answer to that question. Mum is the word.

Chicken

You have many close friends, from a variety of backgrounds, and the rare ability to get along with most people

If this image appears in the bottom of the cup, you spend your free time with others, especially in groups. In one man's cup this symbol showed that he was not a leader or a follower; he was a joiner and belonged to many clubs and activities. If the chicken is seen in the middle of the cup, you are always surrounded by those who love you, and either you have a lot of friends or you could start a friendship cult! If it is seen on the rim, in the future you will be meeting many exciting people.

Chimney

To see a chimney predicts fortunate events

If the chimney has smoke coming out, it is a a good sign of attracting what you want. If it is seen in the bottom of the cup, it shows success soon is here. In the middle of the cup, it is a strong symbol of supreme fortune. If seen on the rim, a strong will has guided you to your present success. I saw this in a cup of a self-made multimillion-aire who came from a humble background.

Cigar

Prosperity will soon be yours, especially with savvy investments

If you want to invest, this is a great time to start. Plan ahead to do what is necessary to make a transaction, in order to make money. If a cigar appears in the bottom of the cup, you spend more time thinking about how you would like to make money than having any actual plan. If it appears in the middle of the cup, then swift business deals are most fortunate at this time. If it appears on the rim of the cup, prosperity is about to pay off with all those dividends. I visited an investment club and saw this image more than once, and in more than one cup.

Cigarette

You have a new plan and you need to follow through

Do not hold yourself back, your idea is a good one, so forge ahead to get what you want. If it appears on the bottom of the cup, you are about to discover that long-ago wonderful idea, the one you cannot let go of, is a good one to implement. If seen in the middle of the cup, others may want to join you in your endeavor. If it appears on the rim of your cup, you are about to take off with a smart idea. A woman for whom I read had this symbol in her coffee grounds for about three years.

First it was at the bottom of the cup and represented an idea but no really strong plan. Then it moved, in another reading, to the middle of the cup, showing she was starting to map out her ideas. Then it appeared on the rim, and she finally got up enough nerve to launch her business. She recently franchised and now has offices in more than ten cities around the world!

Clouds

A creative dreamer; new ideas
could bring fame and fortune

If your feet are planted firmly on the ground, then you are about to fly off. If seen in the bottom of the cup, you need to hold onto childhood dreams of achieving greatness. If this symbol appears in the middle of the cup, take it to the heights of what you desire—you are about to get what you truly want. If it appears on the rim of your cup, others have told you to pull your head out of the clouds and get a real life (aren't you glad you didn't listen?). One young man decided to sell toys and did not take the advice of his family to do something practical (becoming a mailman like his father). He is now very happy that he took his cloud path.

Clover

You and your partner are surrounded by good fortune

Lucky folks such as yourself can't do much better than this. If a clover appears on the bottom, luck has always been on your side. If it is seen in the middle, luck surrounds you. If it appears on the rim, it shows your luck is about to increase. In one couple's cups I saw that they both had this symbol. Later that month they won the lottery!

Cobweb

Triumph over an enemy

Ever wanted to get even and not just mad? Do you want to win the final round? The cobweb indicates a great outcome for those who are having legal problems. If seen in the bottom of the cup, it indicates you are about to overcome a very treacherous enemy. If seen in the middle of the cup, more than one person has tried to sabotage you; it is now time you won over your enemies. If it appears on the rim, you get the last laugh over a secret enemy. I did a reading for a gentleman who appeared to have a score of horrible legal problems. When I spied the cobweb in his cup, I told him that he was about to finish his legal problems and come out the victor. He needed to produce some documents to help his attorney win his case. He did this and he won.

Coins

Money is coming your way;
the more coins the more money

No matter where in the cup the coins appear—bottom, middle, or rim—you are about to receive an increase. If the coins are in the bottom of the cup, you have some old family money coming to you. If they appear in the middle of the cup, then you have made some wise purchases and you are about to come out ahead. If seen on the rim of the cup, long-term planning has made you very comfortable.

Comet

*Coming trouble, watch out for a
neighborhood problem*

Avoid the gossip and pettiness of others. Continue behaving so it is not obvious whose side you are on—stay neutral. If seen on the bottom of your cup, then it means some old feuders like the Hatfields and the McCoys are at it again; this feud is older than the hills, so do not let it concern you. If it appears in the middle of the cup, get ringside seats in your yard, this is going to be a good neighborhood fight. If seen on the rim, future problems with neighbors loom, so settle any small score now.

Computer

A strong interest in technology and in the future, great for making money, especially for those self-employed and/or in high-tech jobs

This is just exactly what it means, no matter where it falls in the cup—in the bottom of the cup or in the middle of the cup, and even on the rim. It all has the same meaning, a creative, computer-oriented or assisted person. Although the computer did not exist in my grandfather's day, I have included this object because I've been seeing it in cups! The book would be incomplete without it.

Confetti

A friend is coming to visit; you will have a wonderful time

Thinking about throwing a party to welcome your friend back? If so, now is the time to plan. If this symbol appears in the bottom of the cup, it shows it has been a while since you have seen a long-lost friend, but you still have many things in common, so do not let past issues stand in the way of renewing your friendship. If seen in the middle of the cup, you're surrounded by people who love you and they'll show it. You have the gift of friendship because you share yourself with others. If it appears on the rim of the cup, plan on sharing all that you have with your friend—time will go by much too fast.

Cow

You will meet an old friend or a former lover

The encounter is not one that you were anticipating, so the surprise will make the meeting even more fun. If seen in the bottom of the cup, you are spending special time with a once-important former lover or even an ex. One woman who comes to see me calls this her "former husband symbol," and they really are like old friends. If seen in the middle of the cup, then more than one good friend will show up. If it appears on the rim, long-lost loves will be united in bliss.

Crab

High ups and downs: try not to be so melancholy; this is a symbol of mood swings

It is difficult to know what you or others are feeling. This can also indicate health problems, time for a thorough checkup. If seen in the bottom of the cup, crab shows spending so much time alone has made you out of touch with others. If it appears in the middle, it shows your health is not good, so take it easy. If seen on the rim, then your moods are affecting others, so try to be more moderate. In one woman's cup the crab showed that she was about to hit menopause and was very weepy.

Crane (bird)

You will live a long life; wherever you see this, it means strength, endurance, and a long life

It is almost as if the person is ageless and has an inner strength that comes from a hardy life. If this bird appears in the bottom of the cup, you will live a long life. If it is seen in the middle of the cup, your strength will endure. If it appears on the rim of the cup, you have many days ahead of you. I see this often in the cups of older people who are real survivors.

Crown

You will benefit from another's will or insurance; this is the source of your inheritance

I never understood why my grandfather left me no money at a time when I was poor. He did leave me three items: a crystal ball, an alchemical set, and a violin from the Gypsy king. It took me a while to understand the significance of the crown that I saw in my cup. It meant that some gifts left behind are truly priceless. If it appears in the bottom of the cup, then an elderly relative will mention you in their will. If seen in the middle of the cup, it shows you will spend much of your inheritance as fast as you get it, unless you use it wisely. If it appears on the rim of the cup, it shows that you are mentioned in a will that you wondered about—you will inherit what is rightfully yours.

Cup

*Be thankful for what you have;
do not ask for anything more*

This is not the time to ask for more in life, it is a time of gratitude or for giving to others. It is not necessary to ask others to repay you—they will in their own time. If this symbol appears in the bottom of your cup, it is time to lie low and not change direction. This can also mean a lack of savings for the future, so you may want to tuck some money away, just in case. If it appears in the middle of the cup, greed will destroy what is yours; do not ask for anything more. If seen on the rim, bills will soon be overdue. Be careful not to ask about them and remain quiet about what you owe.

Cushion

You have a comfortable life,
but sometimes you are too lazy

A woman for whom I was reading had this symbol in her cup. She spent a lot of her time talking about what she did not have instead of what she did have. Also, she had little direction and she was lazy. This is not the best image to have in the bottom of the cup; it implies past comfort. If seen in the middle, a too laid-back attitude can stop you from creating more in your life. If it appears on the rim of the cup this is fortunate; you are going to be very comfortable.

Dagger or Knife

Watch what you say to others;
treachery surrounds you

This is the time to keep your mouth shut and watch; if there is a problem at work you need to be even more careful. If it appears in the bottom of the cup, you hold a grudge from a past deceit (or someone holds it against you). I once had this in my cup when I was young and my grandfather told me to get rid of the chip on my shoulder or the grudge that I was carrying. If seen in the middle of the cup, it shows you spend your time being wary of others, being careful who you trust. When I saw this in one man's cup, it turned out that his wife was having an affair. If it appears on the rim of your cup, be forewarned and prevent future difficulties.

Desk

You need to get all your papers in order, especially your will or other important papers

A woman had complained that her world was in chaos, spinning out of her control. I spied a desk in the bottom of her cup, so we talked about getting organized and cleaning up her papers. The next time she came to see me for a reading I did not see the desk; she had learned her lesson and cleaned up her own desk. If it appears in the bottom of your cup, you are overwhelmed with messiness and it will make you feel out of sorts with your world. If seen in the middle of the cup, then procrastinating only makes you feel worse; get off your behind. If seen on the rim of your cup, it shows projects need to be finished or you cannot move ahead to the next stage in life. Just as seasons change, you may be stuck in the same season forever unless you move on by finishing old projects.

Diamonds

Money and material wealth are on the way, but do not overspend

Enjoy the bounty of your life, but do not max-out your credit card! This symbol normally appears after you have had a long financial drought. It means money that has been a long time waiting will come to you. If it appears in the bottom of the cup, there is sudden money from the past. In the middle of the cup, it shows important people surround you and money is headed your way. If it is seen on the rim of the cup, you must decide where you are going to spend your money. I once got a diamond in my cup before I closed on a book deal. Since then I am always hoping to find more diamonds in my cup.

Dice

*Fortune is changing: it may be
for the best or for the worst*

It is a good idea to step back and be prepared, because some sort of action is about to take place. I recently saw this symbol in a woman's cup. The next day her car broke down and she got a new job. So her fortune was two-fold. If it appears in the bottom of the cup, expect a bittersweet mixture of fate. If seen in the middle, it shows that fate will roll the dice to find out what will truly happen. If it appears on the rim of the cup, watch closely for any signs of future change.

Diploma

*You have neglected a talent you need to nurture;
you may not get another chance to develop it*

If seen in the bottom of the cup, it is a long-awaited secret desire. I did a reading for a woman who did not know what she should do for a living. When I mentioned seeing the diploma, she told me it was her secret desire to go back to school, but she did not know what to study. Since the grounds were in the bottom of the cup it was a past desire, a neglected talent. It turned out she had once been a very good artist. She had decided long ago to be practical and study computer skills. Miserable, she came to me to find out what she should do. (Most fortunetellers see folks who have such questions!) I suggested she consider combining both skills, and she decided to pursue a job as a computer graphic designer. If it appears in the middle of the cup, the skills that you need to develop may be overlooked. If seen on the rim of the cup, work on your talent—it is with you all the time.

Dish

What goes around comes around; your harshness wounds others— you may want to become gentler

In one man's cup this image showed he was mad at the world and took out his aggression by being angry and saying hurtful things to his loved ones. It came to a head when he lost a couple of friends due to his outbursts. His friends came back when he apologized and settled down. If it appears in the bottom of the cup, rash anger has affected the present. If seen in the middle of the cup, it shows what you think and say is powerful, so choose your words carefully. If it appears on the rim of your cup, you may dish out more than you can take; own up and others will forgive you.

Dogs

Trustworthy and loyal co-workers and friends surround you

You are very lucky indeed to have so many people who think so highly of you. Also you are a fair person and you are trustworthy and loyal too. If this symbol appears in the bottom of the cup, you always have a loyal following; you could start your own clique. If seen in the middle of the cup, it shows you have so much support that nothing is impossible. If it appears on the rim of the cup, you are about to do very well with those who think highly of you.

Dress

You will succeed in your plan

Whatever it is that you scheme on and think about will succeed, so be careful what you want to be successful in. If seen in the bottom of the cup, it shows a plan from the past will be successful. Whoever told you that your wildest hair-brained scheme would not be successful was dead wrong. If it appears in the middle of the cup, you are slowly making your plans to unfold what you want. If you are undecided, then prepare to make a decision about what you really want. If it appears on the rim, it shows that now that your plan is set you may have to dress for success.

Drops

A small sum of money or good luck
is headed toward you

This is what my grandmother would call mad money: money you can waste by buying anything you want. If seen in the bottom of the cup, watch out, you are about to spend some money you receive from a surprise source and have the time of your life. If it appears in the middle of the cup, you stash your extra money away instead of spending it, and you are wise with finances. If seen on the rim of the cup, it shows that just when you thought you are going to run short this month, money comes from a very surprising source.

Drums

Success will come because you have great talent; the world needs what you have to offer

When I saw this in one man's cup, it was apparent that he was a very talented artist. He just followed the beat of a different drummer and was frequently told to give up. Fortunately he did not—he is now a very famous musician from Seattle. If seen in the bottom of the cup, it shows you were born with a talent and are a truly gifted person. If it appears in the middle of the cup, you're multi-talented and very creative. It is hard for you to make up your mind what direction to go. If seen on the rim of the cup, success and a blooming talent are headed your way.

Eagle

Reach for the highest heights and your dreams
will come true; nothing is impossible,
the sky is the limit, you can soar anywhere

This is a great image for those who are about to change location. If you ever wanted to move and wondered if your move would be successful, then wonder no more. If seen on the bottom of your cup, it shows you're about to take off with your lofty plans. If it appears in the middle of the cup, it shows noble and strong dreams will come true for you. If seen on the rim of the cup, you will soar with the eagle and know that what you say and do always will lead to where you want to go.

121

Easel

Talent as an artist;
you have a great gift, so use it

No whining when you get this one! You know, of course, you have talent and can use it to create beautiful pieces of art. One woman who had this image in her cup tried to convince me that she had no talent—well, she was wrong and was later very pleased by her first attempt to create art. She was so thankful that she gave me one of her pieces. If this symbol appears in the bottom of the cup, it shows talent is yours from a long time ago. If it appears in the middle of the cup, it shows you can go off in any artistic direction and do whatever you want to do. If seen on the rim of the cup, it is the sign of a true artist with a bright future.

Eggs

A loss of money if broken or a gain in money if unbroken; if the egg is cracked, then be careful how you manage your money

This is one image that you need to incorporate in your readings with a keen look because it can have any manner of interests that may be important. If you have money questions, look at the egg. If an egg appears in the bottom of the cup, in the middle, or on the rim: all have the same meaning, but whether it is with or without cracks is important. A woman who came for a reading had a broken egg in the bottom of her cup, meaning that she was still paying off some bills. A month later she came to see me again. This time the egg was in the middle of her cup and it was cracked. She was undergoing the painful experience of cutting back and learning to manage her money. A year later she came back and the egg was on the rim and was unbroken. By this time, she had a lot better control of her finances.

Elephant

*Assistance from friends or family;
it's a good time to ask for a big favor*

Wonder who is going to help you with your next big project in life or even something simple, like helping you move? An elephant is a helpful image that others will come to your aid, but you must *ask* others for help. If it appears in the bottom of your cup, it shows that with this much support in your life how can you fail? If seen in the middle of the cup, you are on your way to ask others for help and the answer is yes. If it is seen on the rim of the cup, you help others and others help you, great for those who are community-minded.

Envelope

A surprise letter or package will be delivered soon; expect some good news

Many times this is a letter from a long-lost friend or a party invitation. If it appears in the bottom of the cup, someone from your past will be contacting you—could it be a long-lost love? If seen in the middle of the cup, it shows a delivery person could give you more than you expect. If it appears on the rim of the cup, you are about to receive something very nice that could change your life. (Look for initials to clarify who may be involved.)

Eyeglasses

You are not seeing the reality of your situation, be cautious and remove your glasses to get a glimpse of reality

Not that you will see rose-colored glasses in the cup, but you get the general idea about this image. If seen in the bottom of the cup, it shows you need to pay attention to your surroundings, and not sign any papers that you may regret. If it appears in the middle of the cup, take a deep breath and do a reality check. If seen on the rim of the cup, you have spent too much time being unrealistic—that could be in your favor or it may work against you. I saw this in one cup when the person really was inviting disaster, but was optimistic and able to shrug the difficulties off.

Eyes

Attraction and charm; great for actors or actresses, or for going on a interview

Others will listen as you make your point because you have a lot of personal power right now. If this symbol appears in the bottom of the cup, you attract others to you by just being yourself—others find you irresistible. In the middle of the cup, it shows you are surrounded by very fortunate circumstances, use this time to get what you want out of life. If it appears on the rim of the cup, use your charm to get future goals accomplished.

Fairies

Success where you least expect it;
brilliant success comes in small packages

Do not overlook any opportunity, no matter how small
it seems. If it appears in the bottom of the cup, it shows
an oversight that developed into something bigger and
you possibly missed your chance. If seen in the middle
of the cup, it means do not pooh-pooh what you see as
too much work and not enough reward; in the long-
term you will be surprised at the success. If it appears
on the rim, you will receive a surprise and have moder-
ately good success.

Fence

Obstacles are surrounding you,
so think of a new plan to remove them

If you are by nature stubborn you may have put yourself at a disadvantage. If this symbol appears in the bottom of the cup, it is typical of people who sit and wait for opportunities to come to them. When it appeared in one woman's cup (she is in her seventies), she explained how she had few opportunities because she was stubborn. She wanted to marry wealthy so she turned down proposals from men who later became very successful. Because of her "fences," she ran out of time and married out of desperation at the age of thirty-five. Then she blamed her husband for not making a lot of money—it never occurred to her to get a job. She regretted not marrying the first man who asked her. He had a brilliant career and traveled around the world. If it is seen in the middle of the cup, rethink your strategy: why is life not working out as you planned it? On the rim of the cup, it means do not make a decision that can lead you to a dead end—it is easier to start a project than to get out of the fence.

Ferns

Mother Nature is helping you to succeed;
great for gardeners

So you thought that you did not have a green thumb? Well, you are wrong—this is definitely for those who love to garden, or who have thought of gardening. If it appears in the bottom of the cup, it means a lifelong love of nature, you have loved it as long as you can remember. If seen in the middle of the cup, then surrounding yourself with plants relaxes you. If seen on the rim, you need to get out of the house more and enjoy the great outdoors.

Fire

Passion and/or lust, great for lovers
or a magical one-night stand

Also a quick temper is possibly indicated here too—do not fly off the handle in the heat of the moment. If it appears in the bottom of the cup, you are a generally fiery person with much desire for anything that you do. Use that strength to get what you want out of life. If it appears in the middle of the cup, passion could last more than one night, provided you keep your temper in check and watch what you say to loved ones. If it appears on the rim of the cup, and you thought that you had no adventure in life, wait and see what is around the bend.

Fireworks

Your creative spark is about to ignite and take off

A man who came to see me was really very creative, but he had so many talents that he did not know how to apply himself. He constantly wasted his creative energy by not producing anything and feeling sorry for himself. It appeared in the bottom of his cup and also on the top of his cup—it is very unusual to see the same image twice in one cup. In the bottom of his cup, it meant that he was always talented. On the rim it showed that he was finally about to use his creativity to its full extent—no more carping! It was not in the middle for him, showing that he was not then producing any art—thus his frustration. When it appears in the middle of the cup, it shows someone who creates many different things. In one woman's cup, fireworks revealed she was a fabric designer, and that she was pregnant, too!

Fish

Wisdom and blessings are swimming to you; use your gifts wisely

If seen in the bottom of the cup, it means others who are your family, mentors, people of wisdom, or gifted teachers will come into your life and teach you many new ideas. If viewed in the middle of the cup, it shows you are in the position to teach others what you know and what you understand. If it appears on the rim, it shows advancement for those who use their gifts wisely to help themselves as well as others.

Flowers

In general, flowers bring happiness

It does not matter what kind of flower you see, they all mean happiness. If seen in the bottom of the cup, it shows you give as well as receive much happiness from simple sources. A nature lover, you can find the smallest joy in nature's gifts. If viewed in the middle, it shows you are an inspiration to others and you are many people's best friend. If seen on the rim of the cup, it shows true joy comes from giving and you are a helping person as well as giving. There is a happy future for you.

Football

You're about to encounter a large new group of friends

Great for single people who want to meet others who share the same ideas and thoughts and interests. Life is about to change. If seen in the bottom of the cup, a well-established and just plain fun group of friends will soon enter your life. If seen in the middle of the cup, you're surrounded by a close group of friends and "lonely" is a word you seldom use. If seen on the rim of your cup, the football shows that soon you will be swept away with the passions of larger groups—great for those who like politics.

Fork

A sign of a quarrel; think before you speak

If this symbol appears in the bottom of the cup, it means that arguing is great if you are on the debate team—other than that, people will avoid you. Consider the consequences before you act on anything. If seen in the middle of the cup, you need to explain your actions, either in a court of law or in front of others. Write down everything that helps explain your actions and be careful of what you say so nothing is used against you. If it appears on the rim, a volatile situation will set your anger off, so stay cool. I once saw this in the cup of a young woman who did freelance art work. Her client asked her to change a couple of the colors in a project and she exploded in anger. After that she had difficulty finding freelance work for some time.

Fox

You are intelligent and witty;
others ask you to parties

Whatever you want to capitalize on, this clever sign is very auspicious. If viewed in the bottom of the cup, it shows this is a good time to network and go to the places that you have long dreamed of. If seen in the middle of the cup, surround yourself with other bright, witty friends and the possibilities are endless. If it appears on the rim of the cup, then the center of attention is where you will find yourself! My sister always seems to have this image in her cup—maybe that is why she is so popular.

Frogs

*A long and fertile life, great for those
who want to start a family*

If you do not want to start a family, then beware—be careful who you kiss. If viewed in the bottom of the cup, longevity and fruitfulness are often yours. If seen in the middle of the cup, this symbol shows family is important to you, as is spending more time with them. If seen on the rim of the cup, your love of life is infectious to others, so enjoy it.

Fruit

*Sometimes you really wonder about
your family; how dysfunctional are they?*

Do others have the same nutty experiences? This is not always bad, though some of us have unique families and like it that way. For the rest of us—well, look in your cup! If you see fruit in the bottom of the cup and you want some family members to visit (like that long-lost cousin you have been waiting to hear from for years), this shows that the waiting is about to end. If viewed in the middle of the cup, then surrounding yourself with your "eccentric" family is very nurturing for you. I see this one in the cups of people who have very large families and who come in to talk about the other relatives that I saw the previous week—they are woven together like a patchwork quilt. They need each other and they all have some sort of fruit in their cup. They always introduce and talk about themselves as if they are one unit. If fruit appears on the rim of the cup, it means your longed-for, perfect family will not happen, so either make up a family of friends or adopt an organization that serves as a large family.

Garland

Happiness in marriage or in going to a wedding or another blessed event

If you have always been a bridesmaid and never a bride, then you could luck out at the reception. If you catch the bridal bouquet, that's a bonus for you. If it appears on the bottom of the cup, the garland signifies a long and happy marriage. If seen in the middle of the cup, you are surrounded by great friends and others count on you to support them in the celebrations of life. If viewed on the rim, it indicates marriage or some blessed event in the future: you will live happily ever after.

Garlic

*Strength and endurance or the
repelling of an evil person*

Well, if it gets rid of vampires, it is good enough for me!
In the bottom of the cup, it shows a foe posing as a
friend will come back into your life. Bring out the garlic
to send them to the crypt where they belong. If seen in
the middle of the cup, protect yourself from psychic
vampires, but there is no need to hold onto fear. You
will need the strength and endurance that garlic represents to help you. If it appears on the rim, be careful
where shadows lurk around the corner; either take mace
with you or your ninja friend. As with any fortunetelling, it is helpful to know the possible pitfalls in life
so you can prepare yourself. If garlic appears in your
cup, beware and be tough!

Gift

*Thoughtful friends and people
who love you*

If you never knew that you were loved, then you are wrong. Many times the gift comes as a favor or a request that you have mentioned to a friend. In a reading one woman told me she had been reading her own cup and found a gift image in the bottom of her cup. Later that day her neighbor showed up with a bunch of bulbs that he had no use for and he helped her plant them—they both ended up with a gift because now her yard was much more beautiful, and the neighborhood could enjoy the blooms. If it appears in the bottom of the cup, expect a nice surprise. If seen in the middle of the cup, you get many favors because you have such a generous nature. If seen on the rim, the gift shows you can ask and receive what you want from others.

Globe

You are an international person;
you speak more than one language
or you have contacts abroad

I have seen this symbol in the cups of armchair travelers who have friends in other countries. If seen in the bottom of the cup, wanderlust is definitely part of your life. You always have travel brochures around. What do you want to do next? If a globe appears in the middle of the cup, you're planning a trip that will occur soon. Dreams of travel are always with you. If seen on the rim of the cup, travel is in the future. Who said that you never get to go anywhere?

Goats

You take on too much and keep too much
to yourself—bleat it out a little!

"I can do it, let me . . ." you always offer to do too much. This is for the person who volunteers too much and is sometimes resentful of others, or not helpful in trying to do too much. One woman for whom I read had a mother-in-law living with her. The older woman did so much she was almost like a servant or nanny, never complaining until she took on so much she got ill. It was then that my client, the daughter-in-law, started to do her own work. No matter where the goat is in the cup, the person is working way too hard. If it appears in the bottom of the cup, service to others is important to you, but do not spread yourself too thin. If seen in the middle of the cup, it shows you surround yourself with helpers and people who take too much. On the rim, it shows that a major project on which you will work very hard will be coming to the front burner soon.

Golf Club

You are something of a duffer in your life

Leisure time and leisure suits are here—a very popular image for many folks. If seen in the bottom of the cup, then play seems to be part of the past. If it appears in the middle of the cup, then spending time with your friends is what is important to you. If it appears on the rim of the cup, you will be spending more time goofing off in the future.

Gondola

A happy and idle love life

Romance and closeness; you both know how to make each other very happy. If seen in the bottom of the cup, and you are not in a relationship that fits this description, then do not whine; a lover from the past will soon contact you. If it appears in the middle of the cup, you have spent many happy hours just being in each other's company, and others ask you the secret. If seen on the rim of the cup, it predicts a future love for you that will be a once-in-a-lifetime romance.

Guitar

This is an easy one; either you are a musician, have musical talent, or are drawn intensely to music

One person I read for was no great musician, but had such a strong desire to be a musician that the guitar showed up anyway. If it appears in the bottom of the cup, then talent has been with you since day one. If seen in the middle, a humorous and musical spirit is within you. If it appears on the rim, then music greatly affects you and is one of the driving influences in your life.

Hammer

*A reliable and confident person who
can accomplish any goal he or she sets*

No matter what your obstacles in life, you have the
strength and courage to start and to finish what you need
to do, and get what you need out of life. In the bottom of
the cup, the hammer shows long-term desires will soon
turn into long-term achievements. If it appears in the
middle of the cup, others use you as an example of what
one person can accomplish—a born leader. On the rim, it
shows that hard work and determination pay off; you are
soon on your way to enjoying your hard-earned success.

Hand

Great fortune for you if the palm is facing you; if it is the back of the hand, misfortune

How do you tell if it is the front or back of the hand? If you can see lines in the palm, then the hand is facing you. If there are no lines, it's the back of the hand. If seen in the bottom of the cup, then a major decision from your past is about to be made. If it appears in the middle of the cup, then some days you feel that you are on top of the world and other days you feel like the world is out to get you; an extreme mood swing like this is about to push you hard. If the hand appears on the rim of the cup, then you feel you are about to reach the hand of destiny. Ask others for support.

Harp

An eternal romance, poetic and loving

Daydreams can turn into reality. This image showed up in the cup of a hopelessly romantic man. He bought everything in pairs and he married his first love. Not the most practical of men, he was very charming and women would swoon when he walked into a room. If it appears in the bottom of the cup, you have a strong romantic streak and are a very sensitive person. If seen in the middle of the cup, you're easily persuaded by romance and it can lead to some passionate but impractical ideas. If it appears on the rim, then dreams are about to come true!

Hat

A gentleman caller, or a mysterious lady; this very old symbol represents someone trying to cover up information

It can mean that someone will come, but not stay for long. If seen in the bottom of the cup, beware of a person with a hat; it is not to your benefit to give out any information to this person even if it does not seem important. If the hat appears in the middle of the cup, make friends with the hat wearer and he or she will protect you from any harm. If seen on the rim of the cup, then expect a guest who will greatly influence your life.

Haystack

Strive on; you have laid the foundation for a prosperous future

What a resourceful person you are; whatever it is that you collect is sure to pay off big. I have seen a haystack in more than one cup, especially with people who collect trivia items such as Elvis paintings on velvet, or folks who are more serious art collectors. If it is seen in the bottom of the cup, then your hoarding is about to pay off. In the middle of the cup, it shows you should look around for hidden resources; you have some valuables in your possession. If it appears on the rim of the cup, then your savings or collections are about to pay off.

Head

If there are initials nearby, then you think too much of that person; if there are no initials, then you think too much of yourself

Look at in this way—that you cannot get someone or yourself out of your mind. I have seen this in the cup of an older woman who always complained about why this or that did not happen. She could not look past her own life—it was always in the context of a "me, me, me" attitude. If spied in the bottom of the cup, you are flooded by memories. If in the middle of the cup, then you are in a dilemma; so much trivia is in your head you may miss the big picture of what is going on. If seen on the rim, then you are about to be confronted with who you really are in terms of how others see you. This is different from your own image of yourself.

Heart

A lover of life—and others love you too;
if initials are near the heart, it shows a
strong love affair; if the heart is misshapen,
then you are broken-hearted

This is a tricky symbol, so be careful when you interpret it—look closely at how well the heart is shaped. If it is completely well shaped, then you are well blessed in love. If the heart has any lines in it at all, then you really must be aware that either you have been scarred or you might move on in your love life. This is true for wherever it is in the cup. If seen in the bottom of the cup, a long love affair has sustained you through your life. If it appears in the middle of the cup, you're surrounded by love and you are a true romantic. If seen on the rim of the cup, love is on the way. If the image is cracked, heartache is indicated.

Hedgehog or Mouse

Your kindness will be taken advantage of

Start to say "No" for a change. Are you sweet and willing to please, or are you just a bad judge of character when you pick supportive people in life? My neighbor had this in her cup. When I read her coffee grounds one morning, we noticed that she had a hedgehog in her cup. Then she told me about a man she visited with outside of school while picking up her daughter. He, too, had a child in the same classroom and they would talk. My neighbor was enthralled by what a great dad he was and how much he loved children. Even though he was a good dad, he (unknown to my neighbor) abused his wife, and she learned of this by reading his name in the paper after he was arrested. "I guess I am just a bad judge of character," she told me. I think that she is too sweet and sees the best in people without much criticism. If seen in the bottom of the cup, you trust others, much like an innocent child. If it appears in the middle of the cup, it shows you say "yes" so much that you are running out of time for yourself. You're volunteering too much. On the rim of the cup, it shows you are ready to stick up for yourself once and for all—the hedgehog roars!

Hen

Thoughts of home, many times a visit from your mother; if not a visit, then a telephone call at least

On one rare occasion I saw this in a person's cup who was more worried about mothering others than about his own mother. This indicates a homey feeling, apple pie, and mom. If seen in the bottom of the cup, it shows you're nostalgic about your childhood. If it appears in the middle of the cup, you're mothering others and a nurturer; you are probably the first one to show up when a friend is ill. If seen on the rim, it shows you're going home soon or having fond childhood memories that you can share with a loved one—as when my husband showed me the places that he loved best about his hometown. Guess what he had in his coffee cup in the morning?

Hoe

A realistic view on how life is;
if you are discontented, then life
will soon change for the better

This is a person who understands what life is all about, a no-nonsense type of person who does not engage in fantasy or wild schemes. "If you want the truth, ask the person with the hoe in their cup," is what my grandfather used to say. If seen in the bottom of the cup, it shows you were a realistic person from the day you were born, and you did not waste time thinking about what life could be, only what life is. If it appears in the middle of the cup, then others rely on you for support and the ability to help them see what is practical and can-do-able. If seen on the rim, it shows that your long-term vision on how life should be is about to come true!

Horse

If you're a woman, a new man will enter your life;
if you're a man, then a rival will appear; for either
sex, the horse indicates a strong personality

If seen in the bottom of the cup, it is a mood you are
feeling. One of my clients described this feeling as being
swept off her feet when the horse came into her life! You
may experience an overwhelming emotion when this
person enters your life. If it appears in the middle of the
cup, you have something personal at stake here. It may
be a new boss or co-worker—somehow life is more
complicated. On the rim, it shows you should get plenty of sleep; the horse will awaken new powers in you.

Horns

You are a person who is noble
and has great strength and inner wisdom

What is most important here is that you value yourself
as a person. Others admire you, you're a born leader.

When seen in the bottom of the cup, it shows your strength comes from your conviction and your leadership as a child. In the middle of the cup, it means some can see your strength and nobility almost as a sign of arrogance. They don't know who you are. If it appears on the rim, then hardship in your life has made you the strong person that you are today.

Horseshoe

Good luck on a long trip; here is your chance to travel

Where do you want to go? In the bottom of the cup, it shows the places that you dreamed of traveling to and the adventures that you have wanted to have happen on your next voyage. If seen in the middle of the cup, then the sojourn you have been planning is about to change, with a little a twist of good luck. On the rim of the cup, it shows you will be gone longer than you think. I got a horseshoe in my cup right before I went to Europe, and my six-week vacation turned into a six-month stay.

House

If the house is well-built, it means a good home and home life; if the walls are not strong it means misfortune in the home; if the roof is not straight, it involves a bad neighborhood

You need to look closely at this image to determine if the house looks solid. If the house is seen in the bottom of the cup, then this house situation represents your past. If it appears in the middle of the cup, it is your present situation, and if seen on the rim, your future. Home is where the heart is!

Ice Cream Cone

An ice cream cone shows you are in the position of helping a child

It is a very important time not to turn your back, but to be open and offer a helping hand. If seen in the bottom of the cup, then a childhood friend will probably reenter your life. If it appears in the middle of the cup, you are surrounded by people whom you can help. I saw this once in a school nurse's cup. If seen on the rim, it shows a child is reaching out to you. Will you help?

Icicles

Troubles will melt away

What has been causing you problems in life will start to thaw out and evaporate. If seen in the bottom of the cup, then hardships from the past will soon go away. If seen in the middle of the cup, you have more then one problem that will disappear. If seen on the rim of the cup, it shows difficulties will soon pass.

Iguana

This colorful, large lizard means that you are on the fast track to a busy full life, but you are about to have a long rest

It is important that you start to take it easier and slower. If it appears in the bottom of the cup, it shows you have been extremely busy, or not as organized as you would like to be. In the middle of the cup, it shows you should enjoy the rest that you will soon receive—you earned it. If it appears on the rim, it means that it will be a while before life starts to slow down.

Insects

*Start to be more truthful in all relationships—
the other side of this is that others could
be gossiping about you*

No matter how you look at it, this is a wake-up call for a "truth or dare" situation. If others are gossiping about you, then turn away. If seen in the bottom of the cup, it shows problems have been brewing for some time, so take it easy with others. If it appears in the middle of the cup, then politically this is not the best time for you at your work, so watch your back. If it appears on the rim of the cup, tread carefully—you are about to walk into a hornets' nest.

Iron

*Too much work and too many duties;
you need a break*

If the iron is upright, then they have clear insight about work and how to succeed; if the iron is facing down, it means too much work and not enough money. The position of the iron is very important for this interpretation. Where the iron lands in the cup will give you additional insight. If seen in the bottom of the cup, you have worked hard your whole life, and what you own you have earned. In the middle of the cup, it shows you never thought you would make it out of your current position—but you are about to do so. If seen on the rim, congratulations, you are about to succeed.

Island

An isolated feeling, especially if a palm tree is on it and no initials are near it

If the island looks like a particular place (like a Hawaiian island), then the person will be visiting there soon. In a reading when I saw the island and it looked like Honshu in Japan, it was with someone who was visiting us from that country. If spied in the bottom of the cup it denotes loneliness. This means you should speak up; do not remain so isolated, join a group. If in the middle of the cup, it shows you spend your free time with people who are not like you, and you can feel isolated. If it appears on the rim of the cup, it shows you are soon ready to be on your own.

Ivy

If more than one vine, then you are supported by many friends; if only one vine, then you are a person of deep conviction

Ivy entwines you; think of yourself as a tree and the ivy is climbing you. If seen in the bottom of the cup, then you have been fortunate in the friend department. If it appears in the middle of the cup, others support you because of your ideas. If it appears on the rim, you should reach out to others; you have many things to let the world know.

Jars

Great neighbors and fine friends,
you are well-supported in your wildest efforts

No matter what your latest hair-brained scheme is, others join you on the bandwagon. If seen in the bottom of the cup, it shows that whatever your latest scheme is, it will meet with great success. If this image appears in the middle of the cup, it shows you are joining forces with others to get a major job done. If seen on the rim, it shows you should go for a long-term, exciting goal. I found the jar in my cup when I was about to ace a book deal. You see? The coffee grounds knew it before I did.

Javelin

You must put up a fight and defend yourself

If a bully or a lawyer has been giving you a hard time, then this is not the time to wish it away—stand up for your rights. If seen in the bottom of the cup, it shows you are a person who seldom sticks up for him- or herself—you allow others to pick on you. In the middle of the cup, it shows you need to stick up for yourself and for a family member—most likely a child or an elderly adult. Also, you need to learn more about your enemies so you can protect yourself. If it is seen on the rim of the cup, it means that after you stick up for yourself you will never again meet the type of person who has tormented you.

Jellyfish

A false friend is plotting against you; watch out at work, others may want your position

It means you could get stung. Wherever this is in the cup, watch where you step. If seen in the bottom of the cup, then life is about to explode, so tread carefully—powerful jerks are at work to undermine you. If it appears in the middle of the cup, you are in a greater position of power than you think; do not let others get the best of you at this time. On the rim of the cup, it shows you should be strong and have a vision of the future. In the future, be more discreet about who you choose as your friend.

Jewelry

Any type of jewelry that you see in a cup denotes great fortune

If it appears in the bottom of the cup, then you have an interesting family history. I saw the symbol of jewelry in one friend's cup; she then told me that she was descended from an aristocratic family. If it is seen in the middle of the cup, then your great fortune lies in your ability to pick helpful people. If it appears on the rim of the cup, it shows your future is indeed bright.

Jug

You enjoy robust health, or you are learning to take better care of your body

You possess endurance and a strong will, so you can be an example to others. In the bottom of the cup, it shows you realized early in life that health is your greatest wealth. In the middle of the cup, it means you may work in the health field, if you don't already. You are well-educated about health and health-related issues. On the rim of the cup, it shows you will have good health in old age.

Jump Rope

No hurdle is too difficult for you to jump over

Whatever your current challenge is, you will soon meet it with success. In the bottom of the cup, it shows you have the ability to get ahead with any project. In the middle, it means you should keep your mind set and look ahead, it is to your advantage to have a goal in mind. If seen on the rim, it shows your challenge in life will no longer seem so difficult.

Kangaroo

*A true romantic, but a little irresponsible;
be careful who you pick as a lover*

You jump this way or that—everybody looks good to you. You're a flirt at heart and this is how you need to find your way. If seen in the bottom of the cup, then enjoy life and do not get too involved with anything, if only for the moment. If it appears in the middle of the cup, you have a tendency to cry at romantic movies and you are a softy at heart. Beware of being taken in by anyone who resembles a lost puppy. I had a client who took in people instead of animals and, yes, she frequently had a kangaroo in her cup. If seen on the rim, it shows you are an optimist about some of the people you encounter. In short, you could find the good side of even an ax murderer.

Key

Good fortune and wild success:
the best time to follow your dreams,
especially with education

If you wanted to change direction, say from being a teacher to being a hairdresser, or the other way around, then this is your chance. If you stopped your education too soon, then you have an opportunity to start over. I saw this in the bottom of the cup of a young woman who had quit school early and wanted to go back; she was worried about being smart enough. I knew she was, otherwise the key would not have been in her cup. If it appears in the middle of the cup, then everything falls into place. If it seems that you do not have to lift a finger—it is true, you do not have to. Remember that the influences of the grounds do not last long, so take advantage of the opportunities in front of you. If seen on the rim, it means reach for your highest goals—nothing can stop you now.

Kite

A restless soul with little direction

I saw this in a recent reading for a woman who was ready to turn forty. She was very blessed with a good home, marriage, kids, and an interesting career. What was she to do now, she wondered. With the kite in the cup, she was restless and ready to move on with a new project in life—the kite caught her feeling exactly. If seen in the bottom of the cup, you've had a restless feeling for some time; you want to move on, but where to? If viewed in the middle of the cup, it shows you should let go of what is holding you back. Whether people or positions, it is time to soar. If seen on the rim, you don't need direction with a kite in your cup; let the wind of fate blow you away.

Knife

Unless you are a professional comedian, a little dark humor goes a long way; your sarcasm is hurting others

If there is a "C" next to this, it shows unkindness toward children. I saw this in one man's cup where sarcasm was directed toward a neighborhood child. He did not realize that being called names can scar a child for life. Since he thought the neighbor was a likable guy, he had not defended the child. One thing about being a reader is that you can set people straight and I did so by advising him to tell his neighbor to curb his mean-spirited tongue. After his reading, he put an end to this neighbor's harassment immediately. If it appears in the bottom of the cup, it shows you are moving into a "Rodney Dangerfield" type of humor, but he is funny and you are not. If seen in the middle of the cup, it shows some people find you witty, while others avoid your viciousness. If it appears on the rim, you are about to meet your match. If you think you are funny, wait until the person you are about to meet shows up.

Knitting Needles

You need to keep your hands busier
with worthwhile projects; idle hands
are about to bring you down

If a knitting needle appears in the bottom of the cup, then you are just feeling ennui. This is common in people who frequently are bored with their lives. They have little self-interest or resources and they tend to complain of the greatness of others' lives. They always say, "when is something great going to happen to me?" If this image is seen in the middle of the cup, it means too many unfinished projects have you overwhelmed, so either give your projects away to an old folks home where people would be happy to finish your projects, for example, or finish them yourself. Keep busy! If it is viewed on the rim of the cup, then it is not a great time to slack off—better to keep busy doing your work.

Knots

***To see a knot in your cup indicates
that you worry about
the smallest matters***

Loosen up a bit. In one woman's cup where I saw this image, it showed she was full of anxiety, becoming concerned and worrying about small stuff that many of us shrug off. If seen in the bottom of the cup, it shows worries that your past may catch up with you. It's a good time to settle any old-time scores, once and for all. If seen in the middle of the cup, it shows you should not tie up all your energy in day-to-day stuff that simply does not matter. Do you need to get so upset over the small stuff? Relax. If seen on the edge of the cup, you need to unwind; you are very worried about the future.

Ladder

Slowly you have been climbing
to achieve your goals

If a ladder is seen in the bottom of the cup, it shows you are now just starting to put a plan in action. If seen in the middle of the cup, then others need to support you in your endeavor; the more people who can share your enthusiasm the better off you are. If it appears on the rim of your cup, it shows you should start the climb to the stars—you are about to reach your goals.

Ladle

Make sure what you dish out to others you can take when they hand back what they think you deserve

I saw the image of the ladle in one man's cup. He was very sarcastic to others, but he met his match, a co-worker whose sarcasm was very clever, in a mean sort of way. She filleted him with her tongue and he learned his lesson—paybacks are rough. He later told me that whenever he sees a ladle in his cup from now on he is going to keep his mouth shut. If seen in the bottom, then you have a history of this sort of thing. If seen in the middle, you are going to get your due. If it is on the rim, watch what you do now; it will return to you!

Lamb

*This shows a warm and comfortable
home, or you are a person who loves
to take in stray pets or people*

If seen in the bottom of the cup, then your home may
be a sort of neighborhood center. Either the neighbors'
kids come and visit frequently, or others drop in. If seen
in the middle of the cup, it shows others are drawn to
your warmth and your sense of humor. If seen on the
rim of the cup, it shows children and animals love you.

Lamp

*Clear insight into yourself and others;
a wonderful sign for those who work
in the helping professions*

If this symbol is at the bottom of the cup, then you were
born with insight and psychic ability. If it is in the middle of the cup with a line through it, then you were pre-
vented from developing your psychic gift. If no line is

going through this image, then others have encouraged your psychic or intuitive gifts. If it is viewed near the rim of the cup, then you give others insight.

Leaf

A wonderful sign, frequently a sign of good health and robust living if the leaf is whole; a torn leaf indicates poor health

If seen in the bottom of the cup, it shows health issues in the past. Either you learned early the lesson of good health, or you still are working on improving your health. If viewed in the middle of the cup, it shows you are now getting over being ill. This is usually a sign of someone who has pushed themselves so hard that they are fatigued. If there is a letter of the alphabet next to it, then you have been another person's caregiver for some time. If it appears on the rim of the cup, you should pay closer attention to your health. This is a frequent symbol that appears for mothers with two or more children, and it shows mom needs a break.

Lemons

Jealousy toward others, especially people
who seem to have it better than you,
though you do not really know them

If seen in the bottom of the cup, then you compare yourself often to others you do not know, and wonder why they have it so good. In a cup where this appeared, the woman for whom I was reading frequently compared herself to famous people on television. Not only did she sound strange when she talked about it, she seemed to make herself very unhappy as well. If seen in the middle of the cup, it shows you surround yourself with people who irk you. It is time to let go of any pettiness. If seen on the rim of the cup, it shows you should stop comparing yourself to others—everyone has their own problems. Why make mountains out of molehills?

Leopard

*In any area of the cup a leopard
has the same meaning—difficulties
and dangers are ahead of you*

Chances are that you will go overseas, possibly on business. Make sure that you have all your papers in order, especially visa and passport. When I saw this in one man's cup, it showed he did business in a country for which he had only a tourist visa. He had to leave and was not permitted to do business in that country again. If seen in the bottom of the cup, it means do not overlook even the simplest of forms. You could cause yourself trouble at a later date. If it appears in the middle of the cup, look around and make sure that you are not headed for danger. Use caution in everything that you do. If seen on the rim of the cup, watch out for possible dangers in the future. This is not the best time to start a long journey; it may be fraught with danger.

Lighthouse

True leaders have this symbol in their cup; others come to you as if you were a beacon of light, offering hope

You have an amazing ability to help and lead others. Never shrug those abilities off, you are in a unique position to serve others. One man I was giving a reading to was an environmental activist; he stood alone and had great courage. I could see how much he helped others by the lighthouse in his cup. If it appears in the bottom of the cup, it shows you are a person of great ability, so use your gift wisely. If seen in the middle of the cup, it shows others surround you and the way that you conduct yourself is important; your position is so strong that you must use discretion in your decision-making to help others. If it appears on the rim of the cup, then others are reaching toward you and asking for your help—you can help others right now.

Lightning

Inspiration and wisdom; flashes of ideas and insight

I see this image in more cups of computer lovers than anybody else, although computers were not around when my grandfather taught me how to read coffee grounds. Originally, lightning in the cup was for those with great insight. If spied in the bottom of the cup, it shows an original thinker—you can see the other point of view of anything. If it appears in the middle of the cup, it shows great flashes of insight can make you feel like you are a little isolated. Jot down your ideas and use them. If it appears on the rim of the cup, it shows that where you end up with your ideas is up to you. You're definitely a gifted teacher, and can inspire wisdom in others.

Lion

*Fiercely loyal and good-natured;
you are proud of who you are*

Your roar is worse than your bite, but no one should ever back a person like you into a corner. If seen in the bottom of the cup, it shows that others less fortunate than you seek your approval and inner strength. If it appears in the middle of the cup, it shows that as a person of power you have a responsibility to help others less fortunate than yourself. I saw this in one woman's cup and it turned out she was a fund raiser, helping many people by working behind the scenes. So intense was her will that she was able to rally major support for her cause in helping autistic children. If seen on the rim, then be brave—others are expecting you to act.

Lips

Love and romance

It is the same if it appears anywhere in the cup, but if the lips are seen at the bottom of the cup, it has been a while since you have been planted with a big wet one. Even if it is July, you may want to go on out and stand under the mistletoe. If they are in the middle of the cup, it shows a longing for adventure and perhaps a mysterious stranger. It could happen to you. If seen on the rim of the cup, it has a different meaning: love, yes, but keep your mouth closed. It is not the best time to reveal any secrets about your love life.

Lock

It shows a secret that you can never reveal;
so secret that you may have forgotten it

If spied in the bottom of the cup, it shows a skeleton in your family closet, perhaps a relative who was a famous outlaw? If seen in the middle of the cup, it shows you know others' secrets as well as a couple of your own. On the rim of the cup, it shows you have the sharp mind of a detective—you can unlock any mystery.

Luggage

An armchair traveler, or one for real

If your friends tend to go more places than you, you now have the chance to travel in style. In a woman's cup where this appeared it showed that she traveled a lot, but to places that she did not want to go. It seemed that her job was to be a representative of her company. They always sent her on the "dumb city tour," as she was fond of saying. The image of a piece of luggage in her cup meant a lot to her. If the image is seen in the bottom of the cup, watch out for a change in your travel plans. If it is seen in the middle of the cup, the next time a friend asks you to come along on a trip, no matter how short the distance, say yes. If the image is seen on the rim of the cup, pack your bags—you will soon take a trip in style.

Magnifying Glass

You make mountains out of molehills;
everything does not have
to be such a big deal

If seen in the bottom of the cup, it shows past regrets;
occasionally you have had the misfortune of being a vic-
tim. If it appears in the middle of the cup, it shows you
are examining yourself too deeply, so lighten up. If it
appears on the rim, then you are about to question your
lifestyle. Think carefully, examine thoroughly.

182

Medal

*A feeling of accomplishment; others respect
you for what you have accomplished
so wear your badge with honor*

I've seen this in the cups of people who had just finished difficult projects or were promoted. If seen in the
bottom of the cup, it shows you command respect. If it
appears in the middle of the cup, it shows that you can
get others to follow your orders. Be ready to manage
and be responsible. If seen on the rim, it shows that the
older you get, the more respect you will receive.

Mice

*An indication of trouble through
a friend or business associate*

If seen in the bottom of the cup, then you have already
lost a lot in a business deal. If it appears in the middle
of the cup, it shows you are under pressure to secure a
better business deal—don't let others wheedle you. If

seen on the rim of the cup, it shows you will have a lot of problems with a future business partner. Keep this in mind when laying plans.

Money

If it appears as coins, then small amounts are coming your way (see Coins, p. 105); if it appears as a $ sign, then expect more

A symbol next to it will indicate how you earn or will earn your money. A symbol directly across from it shows how you get money from something that is not the type of work you want to do. If there is a symbol above it, it shows you are striving to earn more. If a symbol is below it, then you have many debts. In almost every cup there are these symbols; it is one of the most common things you will see. One woman for whom I read had all these symbols in her cup in one reading. Yes, she had come to see me about money. It was an easy read. She had two jobs: one she liked (represented by an image next to her $ symbol), and another that she did not like, represented by an image across from the $ symbol. She had huge credit card debts (the symbol below the $) as well. Most of all, she wanted to strive for a promotion, represented by the $ above the symbol. She was impressed that I knew so much about her and she loved her very accurate reading. See how truly easy it is? If all of this is at the bottom of the cup, then it is a long-term issue. If it is in the middle of the cup, then events are happening now. If on the rim, then future $ issues are at stake.

Monkey

Manipulation and clever people are at work here

If that used-car deal seems too good to be true, then it probably is. Others may be setting you up as a patsy, be careful of any deals at this time. If seen in the bottom of the cup, it shows that others pull on your heartstrings to have you help them. Maybe it is time for them to do something for themselves. If seen in the middle of the cup, it shows that the monkey person or people can also be helpful and fun, if you do not take their light-hearted jeering to heart. If seen on the rim of the cup, it shows you should beware of false friends.

Monster

A lurking fear, worry, or stress
that you need to face and deal with

Your shadow or dark side is peeping through—time to face the ugly side of yourself! I see this in the cups of people who are either stressed by some nagging problem they are not facing, or oblivious to a negative part of themselves that is hurting others. We all have a dark side; any sort of monster says that yours is now showing. If it appears at the bottom of the cup, then this is an old issue, fear, or dark part of yourself (like a horrible temper or fixation.) If it is in the middle, then it shows now is the time to slay your dragon, whatever it may be. If on the rim, then you need to watch out—you are putting your dark side on something; things are not as grim as you think. Be a bit humble and accept criticism.

Moon

A crescent moon shows you hide your feelings, a full moon shows you tell the world how you feel

Sort of like the Sean Penn and Madonna relationship—she wore her heart on her sleeve (full moon). He hid his behind closed doors (crescent moon). If seen in the bottom of the cup, it indicates a past love, a wistful feeling of the one who got away. If it appears in the middle, it shows you are guided by emotions—you're a moody, sensitive type. If it appears on the rim, it indicates future emotions or changes in how you feel about particular issues, especially if there is another symbol near it. If there is a symbol on the opposite side of the cup, it means you must make a difficult emotional decision. Frequently you see this with those who have marriage difficulties.

Mountain

*You have a major goal in your life—
if the mountain is well formed, you are
about to reach the top; if it is broken,
you need to rethink your strategy*

The goal you picked is not an easy one. Strive to take it one step at a time. No matter where you see this in a cup, it always has the same meaning. If you see more than one mountain then you or the person you are reading for has many goals. If it appears in the bottom of the cup, it shows your goals are long-term and may take a while to reach. If seen in the middle of the cup, it shows you always set your sights on your next adventure and your next goal. In one man's cup where I saw many mountains, it indicated that he had changed his goals and career many times. If it appears on the rim of the cup, it shows you are about to reach your long-term goal, so get ready to celebrate.

Mushrooms

A symbol of fertility

If this appears in the bottom of the cup many times, it represents adult children. If seen in the middle of the cup, it means be careful unless you want to conceive or have another child added to your household (sometimes animals count, like a puppy or kitten). If it appears on the rim, it indicates future children or grandchildren.

Music

Musical notes anywhere in the cup are a symbol of a jolly soul

A lover of life, you are usually what one might call a "fun read." No matter where it is in the cup, music means fun and pleasure. It can be any type of musical note in the cup and if an instrument is near it (like a guitar), then it is a person with musical talent on a particular instrument. If seen in the bottom of the cup, it shows there is a natural rhythm in all that you do. If it appears in the middle of the cup, it shows music is very important to you. Listening to music is food for your soul. If seen on the rim of the cup, it means music will inspire you. Turn on the radio and dance to the music; it will guide you to a different source of inspiration.

Nails

Sturdy, resistant, and as tough as a nails
is what my grandfather used to say
about this image

This is for those who are super strong in life, and bend little to others' wills. If seen in the bottom of the cup, it shows you are a big brother or sister to everyone and you enjoy the role. Some of you may be a little bossy or you enjoy others following your lead. If seen in the middle of the cup, a sturdy, self-reliant individual, you seldom give in to peer pressure. If the image appears on the rim of the cup, others see you as tough as nails.

Necklace

A necklace usually indicates an elderly relative

It can also symbolize that there is a person of authority who is older than you, and you may try to please them. If seen in the bottom of the cup, you should tie up your loose ends with the individual symbolized by the necklace, and he or she will greatly reward you. If seen in the middle of the cup, it shows you're surrounded by those who care about you; it brings you pleasure to please others. If seen on the rim of the cup, it shows you aim to develop positive personality attributes to become more like a treasured elderly relative.

Nest

Homebody, or a lover of children

I saw this in a kindergarten teacher's cup. She had two nests together—one for her own children at home and the other for children in her class. I saw this image once in the cup of another woman who had a houseful of pets—she was like a mom to all the strays. If seen in the bottom of the cup, it shows a nice home is important to you and if you are going to achieve any balance in life your home must be looking good. If seen in the middle of the cup, it shows you make everyone feel like they belong or that they will be secure with you in charge. If seen on the rim of the cup, it shows that a cozy nest is in your future.

Nets

To see a net in your cup denotes
that you will be caught up in intrigue

Do you feel that you are being spied on, or watched by a nosy neighbor? A boss? A friend? If seen in the bottom of the cup, it shows that if you have set up a trap to ensnare another, it will soon work. If seen in the middle of the cup, it means you will soon meet a mysterious person. If seen on the rim of the cup, it shows you will soon be caught up in an unseen force. Hang in there.

Numbers

*Important numbers in your future,
present or past*

For example, in one reading I gave for a friend, I saw
the image of a rock in the middle of her cup (a symbol
of obstacles) and a number "3" next to it—this showed
that there were three problems she was in the middle of
overcoming. Numbers may also refer to dollar amounts,
dates, even times. Numbers are always connected to
other symbols, so they are giving us more information.
If numbers appear in the bottom of your cup, they show
some number and image that influences you from the
past. In the middle, they help describe a current situation, and on the rim they indicate the "how many" or
"when" of future situations.

Nut

Are you a collector? Are you looking for something special to add to your collection?

This is a good-luck symbol of fortune for those who like to squirrel things away or to have some things that they purchase pay off in a big way at a later date. If seen in the bottom of the cup, it shows your prize collection is about to pay off. If seen in the middle of the cup, it shows you have invested wisely and all that surrounds you in your home is worth more than money. If seen on the rim of the cup, it indicates that what you put away now, no matter how little, will pay off in the future.

Oar

An oar in a cup is letting you know
that this is a time in your life
when you will be giving to others

It indicates a sacrifice, for there is really nothing in it for you, but sometimes that is how it is in life. What goes around comes around. This appeared in a reading for a woman who had two young children and also took care of a neighbor's child. The neighbor could not afford day care but had to work. My client did this because she was a good person, not for any other benefit. If seen in the bottom of the cup, it shows you must give to others, such as the needy. If seen in the middle of the cup, it means you may have to give up some of your own anticipated pleasure in order to help others. If seen on the rim of the cup, it indicates that either you sacrifice now or you will give up something in the future. You will be seen as mean-spirited unless you give to others.

Obelisk

Not the best symbol—it indicates
that you must stand alone

I saw this in one man's cup; he had transferred to another city and really had to start over again since his new co-workers weren't very helpful. Having an obelisk in your cup is a lonely sign. If seen in the bottom of the cup, it shows you feel cut off from family and good friends and you are isolated. In the middle of the cup, it shows you need to strike out on your own to make your own place in the world. On the rim of the cup, it shows you are headed for a very lonely place in the world.

Olives

A very old Middle Eastern symbol that is an omen of peace and happiness in the home

The more olives seen, the more joy in the home. If it appears in the bottom of the cup it shows you enjoy a happy home. If seen in the middle of the cup, it shows home is where your heart is. If it appears on the rim of the cup, it communicates a feeling of peace and serenity. A woman I know received this image in her first cup of morning coffee when she moved into a delightful new home.

Otter

A playful happy soul, you can enjoy being totally alone or in a circle of friends

If seen in the bottom of the cup, the otter shows you are the type of person that others invite frequently to parties. If seen in the middle of the cup, it shows you are a carefree, happy person at heart, a whimsical heart-warming type. If seen on the rim of the cup, it shows that the more you let loose, the better life you will have.

Oysters

An ancient aphrodisiac, oysters have
the same meaning when seen
in grounds in the cup: sexy times!

If it appears in the bottom of the cup, it shows passionate, smoldering embers lie deep within your soul. If seen in the middle of the cup, it shows a great time for wild sex. This could be a love fling that is out of this world! On the rim it shows, as my mom use to say, that bad girls get to go everywhere.

Package

A surprise is heading your way,
you may be getting what you want

This is a fun symbol because you always want to find out what surprise could possibly be waiting for you. If seen in the bottom of the cup, it shows a long-awaited gift is about to come your way. If it appears in the middle of the cup, it shows that this is a symbol also of commitment—a sweet symbol—and a relationship can be cemented with a deal. If seen on the rim of the cup, it shows you are very lucky, or you have been kind and generous in the past with others, and you are about to be paid back for all the help and support that until now did not seem to be noticed.

Padlock or any Lock

A feeling of not having many choices in your life, or that others are making decisions for you

I saw this in the cup of a young man who worked in his family's business. He frequently felt that he had too much responsibility; the pressures on him were enormous. Next to the lock in his cup was a book that was open, signifying education. I asked him if he wanted to go back to school and get his degree. He answered that there was nothing he wanted to do more, but his family wouldn't allow it. I suggested to him that if it was work-related they would support him in his efforts. He doubted me, but said that he would try, and called me later to tell me that his family agreed to send him to the university of his choice, as long as he took some courses that would help the family business. In addition to those classes, he was taking others that he liked. If a lock is seen in the bottom of your cup, then hidden secrets from your past are about to resurface. If this image appears in the middle of the cup, then it shows it is not the best time to make any sudden life changes; wait for a better time. If seen on the rim of the cup, it shows you should not be led down the garden path with any false promises—you will find the garden path gate padlocked.

Pail

If the pail is standing upright, business will be good; if it is on its side, hold off on any transaction for the time being

This is a very straightforward "no" or "yes" symbol, especially if you asked any business questions. If seen in the bottom of the cup, you should think deeply about what type of business person you want others to think you are. Do you want to be known as fair or ruthless? Set the tone now. If it appears in the middle of the cup, then before you sign the contract, look at the pail—is it upright or on its side? If this symbol appears on the rim and if the pail is upright, go forward with your plans. If the pail is on its side, stop while you are ahead. I have seen this image in many stockbrokers' cups and I think it always tells them to buy or sell!

Palm Tree

This is really a fortunate sign; it is a prosperous symbol and also shows that you are loved and needed

If there are any good-luck symbols, then this would be considered one of the top ones in coffee ground readings. In my grandmother's cup I read this symbol, which told me that she was very much loved and needed by her family. I have also seen this in the cups of new brides. If seen in the bottom of the cup, it shows good luck and great fortune will be continuous. If it appears in the middle of the cup, it shows that not only are you doing well, but all those around you are thriving too. If seen on the rim of the cup, it shows you are about to have great luck.

Parachute

About to leap off into the unknown
with no real sense of direction; a great symbol
for all of those daredevils out there

One woman who had this image in her cup had just accepted a job overseas. When I interpreted this, she said: "Wow, that is exactly how I felt—like jumping in to the void." If seen in the bottom of the cup: a whirlwind and a spin into the void. If it appears in the middle of the cup, you are game to try something really different—relax and let it go. If it appears on the rim of the cup, that wild, hair-brained scheme that only your best friend knows about is about to become reality.

Parrot

Hello, Hello!!!—there are the talkers
in the world and there are the doers

Right now, you are talking too much and no action is taking place. If it is in the bottom of the cup, then it appears you reminisce too much. If it appears in the middle, it shows you tell others too much personal information. If seen on the rim, it shows you talk too much about what your future will or won't be. Stop yakking and start listening.

Peacock

Beauty is skin deep, but not much underneath

Usually this appears in the cups of people who are focused on their looks and spend much of their money on their wardrobe. My clients who were professional models in Tokyo frequently had this symbol in their cups. If seen in the bottom of the cup, it shows you are a natural beauty. If it appears in the middle of the cup, it shows that beauty and beautiful surroundings are important to you and that you are a person of great taste. If seen on the rim, it shows you are proud and a little vain; you carry yourself as a person of breeding.

Pig

This image has two aspects; on one side a desire that is very important to you will fall through; the other shows that less important desires will materialize

Be grateful for the change of fortune. I saw this in one man's cup—he really wanted to work for a software company, but he did not get to work for the specific company that he wanted. Instead he got a job in a company that he was not too wild about, but it still was a job. I told him that his luck would change if he changed his heart to gratitude and not disappointment. He did, his luck changed, and he later got the job he wanted. If seen in the bottom of the cup, the pig shows a change of fate; what you wanted has changed into a better fortune. If it appears in the middle of the cup, it shows you should chose wisely; the decision that is now facing you will be with you a long time. If seen on the rim of the cup, it means there are two ways ahead for you—which one will you choose?

Puppy

*Get ready for a great party
or other social event*

People you meet will be fun friends, but there is little here that is deep and lasting. If seen in the bottom of the cup, it means take along a lot of business cards, you are about to schmooze and hobnob with some pretty fancy-schmancy people. If it appears in the middle, it shows that things can get out of hand in a playful way and you won't even feel bad in the morning. If seen on the rim of the cup, it shows fun people. Who cares if nothing lasts? Sometimes you've just got to enjoy life.

Pyramid

*Success with your dreams; if you have
more than one pyramid, then you have
more than one desire*

These are always goals that you have worked a long time
to achieve and you have finally reached them. If two pyramids
are across from each other, then you have two
strong goals that directly oppose each other. One client
of mine had this in his cup. He is a classical musician
and a real estate agent, two very different careers, but he
is successful at both. Look near the pyramids to see what
the person is interested in. Any other symbol near the
image is what he or she has been working on for some
time. This will give you more insight into what the person
truly desires in life. If seen in the bottom of your
cup, you're a person of great ability and visionary
desires; you truly go after what you desire. If it appears
in the middle, it shows that after careful thought and
great desire, a major dream is about to unfold. If seen on
the rim of the cup, it shows that what are you about to
achieve is something few others have been able to obtain.

Quail

This is a sign of misfortune;
someone you know
is not entirely truthful

Proceed with caution when confronting this person. If seen in the bottom of the cup, avoid conflict with others. It is best to keep a low profile. If it appears in the middle of the cup, it shows that any new venture will be held up if not stopped completely. Keep calm. If it appears on the rim of the cup, it means that if you work with questionable people, do not reveal much of your plans.

Quill

A sharp tongue and extraordinary wit

When you open your mouth, even the toughest bully will be subdued. If seen in the bottom of the cup, it shows you have always been known for your sense of humor. Since you were a kid you have been witty; others may even mimic your style. If seen in the middle of the cup, it shows you could hold an audience captive. If the quill is spied on the rim, not only do you possesses a gift of gab—you also are a witty writer.

Quilt

A quilt means that the person
has good self-esteem and is able
to comfort others as well as themselves

Always look for an image with lines through it like a blanket. An elderly lady for whom I read had a quilt in her cup. I told her that she was a comfort to many people. She replied, "I sure hope so, I am a minister." If seen in the bottom of a cup, it shows warmth and friendship surrounds you. If it appears in the middle of the cup, you should not cover up such great assets, you are a source of security to many. If seen on the rim of the cup, it shows a colorful, warm, loving person—someone who will do good in the community.

Question Mark

No matter where you find this mark,
it symbolizes the obvious—a question

If seen in the bottom of the cup, it shows a question about the past. I saw this in a charming woman's cup—it turned out she was adopted and was questioning if she should locate her birth mother. If it appears in the middle of the cup, it shows a proverbial question. Soon fate or life will give you the answers. If seen on the rim of the cup, it shows your question is: what should I do now? Look at the other symbols next to the question mark; this will tell you what to do.

Rabbit

*A fertility symbol, it can also be translated
into the beginning of creation, the seed
of a fertile idea, or the start of a new project*

These and similar concepts can be represented by a rabbit. I have seen this symbol in many cups of artists who are changing direction in their art. If seen in the bottom of the cup, it shows there has been no creativity for some time. If it appears in the middle of the cup, it shows someone who has started and stopped at their art. Maybe they should start again. If it appears on the rim of their cup, it shows there are many creative ideas—where to start next?

Rainbow

Good fortune and happiness

If it is near the handle, it shows long-term goals will soon be reached, especially a heart's desire that you never dreamed would materialize. When I saw this in one young woman's cup, I knew something good was going to happen to her. She told me that she applied to Harvard's MBA program on a dare—her husband told her she could never make it, so she tried and was accepted! The rainbow is a symbol that dreams do come true, even with obstacles in the way. If seen in the bottom of the cup, it shows a ray of hope will come your way. If it appears in the middle of the cup, it means great fortune—look for the pot of gold. If it appears on the rim of the cup, it shows you should follow your dreams and be bold about your heartfelt desires.

Rake

*A happy home—you spend much time just
enjoying your living space, the people, objects,
the inside and outside of your home*

I also have met many men who spend a lot of time in
their garages working on stuff—with this image in their
cups I can see why. If seen in the bottom of the cup, you
will reap what you sow. If you remember that, you will
make clear decisions. If it appears in the middle of the
cup, the rake shows a very industrious person—if I
need anything done I will give you a call. You're a project person who gets the job done and does it well. If
seen on the rim of the cup, it shows money is headed
your way. Literally, you will be raking it in.

Ring

Marriage (if it is solid); if the ring is broken, then it shows either a divorce or that the marriage is on a rocky ground

Look to see if there is a another symbol next to it; that would be a clue to the type of relationship it is. If you see more than one ring, then there has been more than one marriage. If the ring is especially strong and dark, then it is a strong marriage; if the ring is weak, then there are misgivings about the marriage. If seen in the bottom of the cup, it shows a marriage in the past. If seen in the middle, then it shows it is a marriage that you are currently concerned about. If viewed on the rim, it shows a wedding in the future.

River

*This also can be read as wavy lines;
an emotional response to whatever
the person is feeling at the present*

If the river has many bends, then the person is going through a very emotional time. If there are a few bends in the river, then you tend to be moody about things now. If the river has only two bends in it, then this is a person who is divided in feelings. Where the river is also helps define the meaning. If viewed in the bottom of the cup, it means that holding on to past hurts can stop personal development. If seen in the middle of the cup, it shows you have deep feelings. If it is seen on the rim of the cup, it shows you tell the world your feelings. I have seen this image many times in a variety of cups. When you see this, always ask clients how they are feeling—then bring out a box of tissue.

Road

*You are about to step forward into the world
of travel and adventure*

Be brave and do not worry. My niece got this in her cup
when she was about to move overseas with her family. If
seen in the bottom of the cup, it shows that you once
were an armchair traveler and now you will get to experience what you wanted to do for a long time. If viewed
in the middle of the cup, it shows wanderlust is in your
heart and on your mind. If seen on the rim of the cup, it
shows you are ready for a big adventure, with a major
life change.

Rocket

*A big idea is about to take off;
you are headed for the stars*

If the rocket has a line next to it, or another image, it is
best to rethink strategy and hold off on changes for the
present. If seen in the bottom of the cup, it shows you

have mental and physical energy to burn. If seen in the middle of the cup, it shows you have the nerve and flexibility to move forward fast. If it appears on the rim of the cup, it signifies that you should hold on—you are about to get an offer that is out of this world.

Rocks

Misfortune—an obstacle in your path; instead of working it out, be like a river and flow around it

Most of the time a rock is an image that represents a person. When I saw this in one woman's cup, she was about to embark on a promotional trip to launch her new book. She got involved with an unscrupulous promoter who wanted to cheat her out of her money, so when she came to me for a reading she got quite a few rocks in her cup. I told her to go around the rocks. Some things are like rocks, and it is the same with some people; no matter how hard you try you sometimes cannot work things out with certain people. She "went around the rocks" and avoided the troublemaker as I advised her to, and she had a very successful trip. If seen in the bottom of the cup, rocks indicate an unfortunate past. If seen in the middle of the cup, this shows hardship surrounds you. If seen on the rim of the cup, it means you may endure some misfortune.

Rope

This is an obstacle: if the rope is tied
it means health problems;
if the rope is in a circle it shows
difficulties with finances

If seen in the bottom of the cup, the rope shows long-term health and/or financial problems. If seen in the middle of the cup, you should tie up loose ends to improve health and finances. If viewed on the rim of the cup, it shows you are headed for health or money obstacles; be careful to avoid the most obvious ones.

Sailboat

A lover of the sea and sky; an unconventional, wanderlust type who is also a lover of the finer things in life

Expensive tastes and intelligence figure into the personality type of individuals with this image in their cup. If seen in the bottom of the cup, it shows a friend from afar is soon to appear. If it appears in the middle of the cup, it shows you live life with gusto and enjoy many types of people. If seen on the rim of the cup, it means you should relax; you are about to enjoy life to its fullest.

Saw

Difficulties to overcome and resolve—wherever it is in the cup, it is not the best symbol

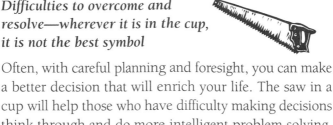

Often, with careful planning and foresight, you can make a better decision that will enrich your life. The saw in a cup will help those who have difficulty making decisions think through and do more intelligent problem solving. If it appears in the bottom of the cup, difficulties have been surrounding you for some time, so it is best to make a decision and try to overcome the weakness in your character. If seen in the middle of your cup, it shows you should cut through any problems on the back burner. In Tokyo, when I read for my clientele, it is not unusual to find a saw in a cup at the end of the year. Japanese custom is to complete all unfinished business— all debts are paid off at the end of the year so they can start the new year fresh. The saw in the cup represents resolving all and starting with a clean slate. If seen on the rim of the cup, it means to make sure that you have planned carefully for the future.

Scissors

A warning of false friends—do not give away too much private or personal information, especially to new friends

Many times it also indicates that a move will be taking place soon. If it is seen in the bottom of the cup, watch out for new neighbors, unless you want them to tell others a lot of personal information. If it appears in the middle of the cup, it shows you have picked friends who are not supportive right now, so you may want to re-evaluate your choices. If seen on the rim, move slowly; you are about to be deceived. This is a good time to be paranoid. Trust no one with your deepest darkest secret.

See-Saw

A relationship that will not be long lasting

When I saw this in a woman's cup, I told her that she was in a turbulent relationship that might not last long.

She said, "Oh, that is my husband—well, on paper he is my husband. We are having a problem with immigration so we will have to live together for some time. I am not happy about this at all—in fact, that is why I wanted a reading." This image in the bottom of the cup shows a moody partner or that you are moody. In the middle of the cup, it asks the question: do you want your relationships to go up or down? There is no in-between with this symbol. If seen on the rim, you need to ask yourself which direction you want your relationships to go. This is a great time to make a lifelong personal choice.

Sheep

Careful planning has paid off and you are on the way to achieving a plan that you hatched

Wonderful for any wild, hair-brained scheme. If you ever wanted to cash in on an invention or business idea, this is the time. If seen in the bottom of the cup, it shows you have been planning on making a move in a business deal for some time; this is a good time to implement your plan. If seen in the middle of the cup, it shows you are well protected from having your "plan in action" go by the wayside. If seen on the rim of the cup, it shows you may make a lot of money with your new idea.

Shell

Creative and artistic; you're able to communicate to others in a meaningful way

This shows a flair for decorating and a lot of panache. A woman who had this in her cup looked so familiar to me that I thought I was mistaken. After the reading I remarked that she looked like a famous Seattle musician. "I am," she replied as she took off her sunglasses. This is really an age-old symbol of femininity. If seen in the bottom of the cup, it shows you have always been creative, since the day you were born, so use your gift. If seen in the middle of the cup, it shows you can make any room look great, you have a true gift for designing. If spotted on the rim, it shows that the longer you live, the more creative in life you'll become.

Ship

Get ready for a major positive change in your life

Even those who resist change will welcome it soon. If seen in the bottom of your cup, it shows that just when you think your life will not change for the better, it does; enjoy your new-found fortune. If seen in the middle of your cup, it shows you have started to take the steps necessary to bring around change; it will be a vital and uplifting turn of events. If spied on the rim of the cup, it means brace yourself—your ship has finally come in! Are you ready to sail off into the sunset?

Shoe

If the shoe is well formed then you are in a comfortable position, well liked by neighbors and friends

If the shoe is not well formed, then the opposite is true. If it appears in the bottom of your cup, it shows you can change the way others perceive you. If seen in the middle of the cup, it shows that if the shoe fits, you wear it. You have strong supporters and strong enemies—you are a person of power. If seen on the rim of the cup, it means pay attention to what others say about you.

Snails

A snail's pace will get you there,
but in no hurry

If seen in the bottom of the cup, then you have not reached your potential. If it appears in the middle of the cup, then you have slowly moved toward what you want, especially if it is near the handle. It shows you have not picked an easy road in life. If seen on the rim of the cup, it shows you are moving toward your long-term goal, and you will reach it in the end. Whenever I see the snail near the rim, I always tell the client "Congratulations!" They know what I am talking about.

Snake

You will need to make a very intense decision; wisdom is on your side

The snake symbolizes wisdom and strength and all responsibility too. If seen in the bottom of the cup, it shows you have made many decisions for others and have influenced many people. If it appears in the middle of the cup, and near the handle, then you have made a life or death decision. If the snake appears on the rim, then it shows you have regretted a decision in the past. Sometimes the snake symbolizes procrastination about making some decision.

Spade

A obstacle is in your way and it's preventing you from finding out the truth in life

It is also an indication that you should take everything slower and watch out on a voyage. It is not a great time for taking risks. If seen in the bottom of the cup, it shows you have talked yourself out of making some choices that could have greatly benefited you. Normally those choices are education related. If seen in the middle of the cup, it shows that life has been giving you little choices. Do not despair. If it appears on the rim of the cup, then you should prepare yourself to slow down a little. Most of the time when it is on the rim, it indicates that the person is headed for financial problems and is a little too carefree with charge cards. A warning like this can help you avoid misfortune.

Spear

Worldly success and enjoyment—
a wonderful symbol, especially on the rim

If the spear is pointing up, the future looks bright. If the spear is pointing down, what you thought would happen will happen, but in a slightly different way. If the spear is straight, then you are very leveled-headed and others expect you to help them. If seen in the bottom of the cup, you have had an interesting childhood—played out in the direction of the spear. If the spear appears in the middle, it shows you are self-directed and on your way to bigger and better things. If seen on the rim, it shows the future is mighty rosy.

Spider

My stockbroker clients love this symbol for it shows great success in finances

A woman in Tokyo had this in her cup, on the rim near the handle—this is always a very strong location. She called me later to say that she had made a lot of money from some investments. If the spider is seen on the bottom of the cup, then long-term ventures are the best for you. If it appears in the middle of the cup, then diversity is the key for finances. Do not put all your eggs in one basket, or your spider in only one web. If the spider is seen on the rim, you can now safely take a financial risk, like contacting a stockbroker, or try buying a lottery ticket—you never know.

Spiral

Just when you think you can't understand something— wham, you figure it out

This is the "eureka!" symbol. That piece of information that you needed to make a decision has finally come to you. A spiral is a common image in a student's cup, or in the cups of those who are learning something new. If seen in the bottom of the cup, it shows that the truth will soon be understood. If it appears in the middle of the cup, it shows you surround yourself with like-minded individuals and an important matter will soon be clear. If viewed on the rim of the cup, it indicates that you have figured out that long-burning question inside of you—now what will you do with the information?

Squares

*Plan differently and go around
what is bothering you in life*

Look at a square as if it is an obstacle in the path. Get support from your loved ones and take a detour. If it appears in the bottom of a cup, then it shows you have stopped yourself from getting ahead. Usually it means an early marriage to the wrong person, or picking the wrong friends, or some basic problem in your character that you need to work on. If the square is seen in the middle, then you should ask others for help to get you through any problems that you may be having. If it appears on the rim, then it shows that careful planning and close friends will get you through the most difficult places in life.

Squirrels

*Hard work is not a stranger to those
with this image in the grounds*

It is easy to get side-tracked and forget what it is that
you want most. An example is the client who was
always going in too many directions at once. Even
though she was a hard worker, little was accomplished,
for she seldom completed anything and always left
everything half-done. I told her that she needed to drop
this bad habit, go back and pick up the worthwhile
projects and quit the others. There is no failure in
changing your mind, I said. She agreed and she went
on to feel better about herself after stopping her "squir-
rely" behavior. If the squirrel is seen at the bottom of
your cup, then it shows you have picked more than
one major idea on which to focus in life. If it appears in
the middle, it shows a very busy time for you. On the
rim, it shows you are a person who is about to begin a
big project.

Stairs

A promotion or a change in work that will be for the better

I did coffee ground readings at a party for a large corporation. Many of the people who were there had the stairs in their cups, but many also did not. This was before a large layoff was announced. Most of those who had the stairs continue to work for the company; most of those who did not have the stairs were laid off. If the stairs are seen on the bottom of the cup, then it shows you have had a long climb to the top. If the grounds are seen in the middle of the cup, then it shows you have been passed over for a promotion, but you may soon have another opportunity. If the stairs are seen near the rim, it shows you are on the way to a promotion or advancement of some sort.

Star

A good-luck symbol of hope and dreams that do come true

This is a beautiful symbol for those of us who are dreamers. If seen in the bottom of the cup, it shows the wish that you have had close to your heart is about to come true. If it is seen in the middle of the cup, then it means you should make a wish—it has a good chance of succeeding. If it appears on the rim of the cup, you can reach for the stars—your dream will soon come true.

Sun

A strong personality—others are drawn to you and your bright spirit

You have a lot to offer—this is an especially good sign for teachers and other leaders. If seen in the bottom of the cup, it shows you have always developed a relationship with children, and others see you as a leader. If the sun appears in the middle of the cup, it shows a strong charismatic personality and that others who are equally powerful are in your life. If seen on the rim of the cup, you are more intense the older you get.

Swing

A change of plans will happen soon—
it is really unexpected and it could go either way

If the swing is seen on the bottom of the cup, then you have had a problem in the past making choices and plans. If the swing is seen in the middle of the cup, it shows you will have a couple of small changes coming up. If seen on the rim, it shows a swift abrupt change. This is a good symbol for those who feel stuck in a rut, or those who thrive on change.

Tack

*Smart and quick-witted, you can talk
others into anything*

You are known also for your sarcasm. You're a talented writer and intelligent. Watch it though; I had one client who had a few of these in his cup and he also had a black eye from not watching his mouth. If the tack is seen in the bottom of the cup, it shows you have a great gift for sales and you are as sharp as a tack. If this grounds symbol is seen in the middle, it shows you are intelligent in many subjects, and your fortune is to make a living with your words. One client I had, a speech writer, had this in his cup. If it appears near or on the rim, it shows you are soon to realize what a great gift of gab you really have.

Tambourine

Inconstancy in a relationship

If it is a big romance, the relationship will be a very exciting one with plenty of intrigue and passion, and then no phone call the next day. What is attractive in a relationship like this is that it is so exciting. If seen in the bottom of the cup, it shows you gave up on one love affair to head in another direction, but it is one affair that you really have not been able to forget. If it appears in the middle of the cup, then it shows that you desire to be caught in a whirlwind romance. If it is seen on the rim, it shows a coming exciting relationship, either in love or friendship.

Tassels

Get ready for company and you can be sure
that you will all share a delightful time together

These are the types of images that you enjoy having. If the tassels are seen in the bottom of the cup, then it will be old friends or an older relative like a grandparent. If the tassels are seen in the middle, then it shows your guest will not stay as long as you would like. If the tassels are seen near the rim, then a long-lost friend will come to visit, especially if the image is near the handle. If it appears across from the handle, near the rim, a mysterious guest will reveal a secret.

Telescope

What you believe the future
will hold for you

You should only attempt to implement things you really want to come true. In one person's cup, a telescope was in the middle, so I asked him if it meant that he was searching for something that was relevant to his life. Bingo! He wanted to be a screenplay writer and to be offered millions of dollars for his first script. He was middle-aged and had not written anything since high school. His goal, although not impossible, was not an easy one. He talked as if it was a done deal and that if he just talked about it, then he would be discovered by Hollywood. I told him that saying you want to be a screenplay writer did not mean anything unless you wrote. He started to get clarity on the telescope image and to focus into what he really needed to do in order to make it a reality. This is what is important in a reading—to give insight into a problem and to offer solutions to it. If it is seen in the bottom of the cup, the telescope shows your visions have always been far-reaching. As a child you were probably labeled a dreamer. If it appears in the middle of the cup, then it shows you are searching for a different reality. If it appears on the rim, then it shows you are a person who is going to reach for the stars to achieve your dreams.

Tiger

*A tiger, like any of the cats, is a warning sign
that you need to find some inner strength
to get on with what you are doing in life*

It is like taking a deep breath before you jump into the depths. I have seen this symbol in the cups of more people who were going to fight for a cause they believed in than any other type of symbol. It is the inner strength that we draw upon to get what we need in life, a source of courage. If the tiger appears in the bottom of the cup, it shows you had a ferocious past. If seen in the middle of the cup, it shows you are often in the position of having to defend yourself. If it appears on the rim, it shows you are about to get what you want because of sheer cunning, strength, and vitality.

Tomatoes

A comfortable and desirable image—
this person has the ability to achieve
a comfort level in his or her home
and in personal relationships

You are lacking for little, more because of a great attitude than for any other reason. You see what you have and not what you do not have. One very loyal client I often see always gets a tomato in her cup. It is almost always there, no matter where it lands in her cup. At the beginning of every reading she asks me if her tomato is still there. "Of course it is, because you are comfortable!" I say. We always chime in together on this. It is true she has always had a good life and has had people who love her, and has always lived in the same home since childhood. She has never lacked for a thing. If it appears in the bottom of the cup, it shows you had a comfortable past. If it is seen in the middle, it shows you are comfortable with your life now. If it appears on the rim, it shows you will be comfortable in the future.

Tornado

*Turbulence in your life—you're easily
swept up with your emotions*

A feeling of being almost out of control, especially if you find yourself going in a new direction. It is particularly tough for a person who is not flexible. With a tornado in your cup you need to bend in a situation—do not expect everything to go your way. It will soon blow over. A woman came to see me who was getting a divorce from her husband and wanted everything in the divorce to come out in her favor. I told her that even though she wanted everything to turn out perfectly for her, she was going to have to give a bit. (Although they had no children and she had a job, as did her husband, after ten years of marriage she wanted the house and all their belongings and no debts.) "He can pay it all off," she cried. Her anger was stopping her from looking at the situation realistically—she lived in a state where everything is divided fifty-fifty. She did not like her reading, but called me later to tell me that her lawyer told her the same thing—that she should calm down and see a counselor. It was helpful for her to be told that she had a tornado in her cup so she could look at her desires more realistically. If it appears in the bottom of the cup, it shows a turbulent past. If seen in the middle of the cup, it shows emotional needs are currently at their height. If it appears on the rim, you should prepare yourself for a "storm."

Treasure Chest

This is about revealing the glory that is you!

If the chest is open and jewels are in it, then this is a very strong symbol, but if the chest is closed it means you are not ready to show yourself to the world. If seen in the bottom of the cup, it shows your past will be revealed. If you have anything that is covered up, it will be exposed—often an unfortunate image for politicians or television preachers! If it appears in the middle of the cup, it shows you will start to have some insight into why life is not going the way that it is planned.

You'll begin to shine. If seen on the rim, it shows you are about to discover what a terrific person you are and so will others. Prepare to be glorified.

Trees

Strength and nobility is what others see in you

No matter where you are on the social scale, you hold your head high and command an aura of importance. If a tree appears in the bottom of the cup, it shows you are a person who has overcome difficulties, and that you are a person of strength. If seen in the middle of the cup, it shows that others seek your inner strength and ability to command. If it appears on the rim, then it shows you are a person who knows your true strength in the world.

Turtle

*Move slowly, with purpose and
dedication, and you will succeed*

Just make sure that you pick one goal at a time, not
many. Others may see you as inflexible. This is not
true—you have a steadfast purpose in life. If the turtle
appears in the bottom of the cup, it shows that it has
paid off for you to go forward in life with a single goal.
If seen in the middle of the cup, it shows you have gone
with what you want in life with practical consideration.
On the rim, it shows success will soon be yours if you
are steadfast and focused.

Umbrella

Shelter from obstacles, and safety from financial woes

Most of those who have this in their cups are financial planners of some kind and are able to save for a rainy day. It also can be a sweet romantic encounter—only you must make the first move. If an umbrella is seen in the bottom of the cup, it shows you have learned from the past that you can move forward only if you save your money and apply it wisely. If it appears in the middle of the cup, it shows that you should start to plan what you want for the future; you have options now and some protection. If seen on the rim, it shows you are protected from obstacles.

Unicorn

So what is it that you really fantasize about?

No matter how unusual your daydreams may be, they have a chance to finally materialize. One woman who had the unicorn in her cup was looking for a place to open up her new store—the next day she found just the right building. In the bottom of the cup, it shows that as a child you were called a daydreamer, when you were a teenager a loner, and as an adult a visionary. You must ask yourself: What is your dream today? If seen in the middle of the cup, it shows that many visions, dreams, and fantasies make you a very interesting person. If seen on the rim, mystical and strong dreams pull others into your world—you are hypnotic.

Urn

*Psychic ability—for you, any of
the psychic sciences are easy to learn
and you can conjure up
or materialize what you will*

In one man's cup, this symbol pointed out that he was really a brilliant astrologer. In the bottom of the cup, the urn shows that since childhood you have possessed psychic gifts. If seen in the middle of the cup, it shows you need to activate your sacred power; it is not being used to its full potential. If it appears on the rim, then the urn is an amazing image of psychic development, especially for those who desire to be more psychic.

Vase

A secret is to be revealed

A client of mine had this in his cup—he was a professional by day and a drag queen at night. He had a secret lifestyle only known to a few: his lover, his mother, and me. It signifies that kind of secret, something that is almost a hidden idea about who you are. It is a great image for those who work in the foreign service or law enforcement, or in some sort of secret activity. If it appears in the bottom of the cup, you should watch out for problems that may surface. I knew a woman who had this in her cup who later went on to marry her first cousin. If seen in the middle of the cup, it shows you hold the secrets of your life deep inside you. If it appears on the rim, it shows you are about to be discovered—your true identity will be revealed

Vegetables

Any type of vegetable is a symbol of prosperity, and most also can be a symbol of fertility

If the vegetable (or group of vegetables) appears in the bottom of the cup, it indicates bounty and the ability to have a long and prosperous life. If vegetables are viewed in the middle of the cup, it shows you have made wise choices, and what you possess you have earned. Your prosperity will continue. If it is seen on the rim of the cup, wealth, comfort, and longevity will be yours.

Violin

*An exotic stranger who sweeps
you off your feet; a wild, passionate,
and whirlwind romance*

Usually the person is foreign, or someone you meet in
an exotic country or place. In one cup where I saw this,
I asked the woman: "Where are you planning on going
for vacation?" She said she was flying to Turkey. I told
her to be prepared to have a wild, romantic encounter
with a handsome man she would meet at the airport.
She told me she doubted that—she just wanted to see
archaeological sites. She called me after she came back
with the news that she had met a man at the airport as I
said, and that they had a wild romantic encounter. It
was much more memorable than seeing some digs. If it
appears on the bottom of the cup, it shows you have a
very romantic nature. If seen in the middle of the cup, it
shows you are to have a secret meeting with someone
you barely know. On the rim, it shows you should get
ready for loving!

Volcano

*Family problems that have not been resolved
will now start to come to a head*

Expect that there will be some real anger about an issue
that you have little control over. I have seen this image
frequently with those who are about to fight over a will
or some personal effects. If it appears in the bottom of
the cup, it shows that family problems that have never
been resolved will blow up. If it is seen in the middle of
the cup, then you are about to be in the middle of a
family disagreement. If it appears on the rim, you
should watch out—the fuse on someone close is lit and
they're about to blow.

Wagon

*This symbol has a similar meaning to the car;
it has to do with normal transportation*

In the older tradition this symbolized a move to another city. Now, with so many commuters living in the suburbs and working in the city, the meaning has shifted to this sort of movement. I doubt it would make a lot of sense to say to someone who got this that they were traveling to another city. They probably would answer the obvious, that they commute. If it is seen at the bottom of the cup, however, the meaning is very different. It has to do with being a little homesick for another city, or having the desire to move to another place. If it is in the middle, it shows you are a commuter, or spend a lot of time driving around. If seen on the rim, it shows you are about to make a move of some kind, or are changing your commuter pattern. If the wagon has poorly formed wheels, then anticipate car or commuter trouble. Last time I got this in my cup, I found that I had left my car lights on all night, resulting in a dead battery—sigh!

Weasel

This is the symbol of a person who is trying to use you; proceed carefully

Beware of people who try to befriend you for no reason that you know of. If the weasel is seen in the bottom of the cup, it means you should take it easy with a person from your past who will contact you again. In the middle of the cup, it shows that people who are currently in your life may use you (hint, look for a letter near the image to find out who the weasel really is). If seen on the rim, it shows someone in the future that you mistrust will contact you. Watch out.

Whale

A small gain in your money—
it is like a small increase in work

The important idea is that it will lead to something much bigger than you thought it would. If seen on the bottom of the cup, it shows a slow increase in friendship and money. If it appears in the middle, it shows you have the support of others to get done what you need to do. If spotted on the rim, it shows you will find that "small is large" in many areas of your life.

Windmill

An image of sitting still while the wind
tries to blow you about

Of course you must remain true to yourself and not let others try to influence you so much. If seen in the bottom of the cup, it shows that in the past you had to remain still and firm against all odds. In the middle of the cup, it shows you are trying to find your own pace, not moving too fast or too slow. If this image is seen on the rim of the cup, it shows you are caught up deciding which would be the best way for you to move forward. This is a great time to sit tight and see what happens.

Wolf

A wonderful symbol of strength and courage

You have a strength about you that few can match. When I was reading for a woman named Ellen, she had this symbol in her cup, showing that she really was a person of great courage—she had cancer and survived. Although still recovering, she knew this symbol would get her through. She loved this totem and bought some objects that had wolves on them to help her remember that she had courage and strength. If it appears in the bottom of the cup, you are a person who was born strong, or some might say opinionated. In the middle of the cup, it shows you are a person who makes it through life with determination and spirit. If it appears on the rim, it shows you are about to find out where your courage truly lies.

Xylophone

A very talented individual

I have seen this image in cups, although not frequently. A xylophone indicates a person with many talents and the ability to change and adapt in creative ways. When it appears in the bottom of the cup, a xylophone indicates those who have been flexible most of their lives. If seen in the middle of the cup, it shows you are a complicated person with many talents—use them now. If seen on the rim of the cup, it shows you are about to hit your creative stride.

Yarn or String

If it is in a ball, with little string hanging off,
you are doing too much at once; if there is
a long string hanging off, then you
are very overworked

It is a good symbol, though, if you like to keep busy with projects. If it appears in the bottom of the cup, it shows you are a doer in life, not just a thinker. If seen in the middle of the cup, it shows you are involved with many projects and that your platter is full. If it appears on the rim, it shows you are about to start some far-reaching, important work that will benefit many.

Yoke

A feeling of being held back or being stifled—being kept away from what you desire, a feeling of being frustrated with your lot in life

This appeared in one woman's cup, showing she had a job that kept her pretty straight and narrow. What she desired was a change of pace and the chance to do something really different. By staying on her path, keeping an open mind, the yoke eventually led her to where she wanted to go. If seen in the bottom of the cup, it shows you remain focused on future goals. If seen in the middle of the cup, it shows others want you to take jobs that are boring. If seen on the rim of the cup, it indicates that, whatever you feel is holding you back, this is not the time to move forward.

Zebra

You're stopping yourself from enjoying your friends

It could be you or someone else who is a little too stubborn—or frequently it is a co-worker who is driving you crazy. Ask yourself this: have you ever seen anyone ride a zebra? No, they are too uncooperative. If it appears in the bottom of the cup, it shows you have spent too much time stopping yourself from enjoying life, or you could have a child in your life who is a difficult person. If seen in the middle of your cup, you have spent too much time fighting with your peers. If it appears on the rim, it shows you are about to meet your match in stubbornness.

Zeppelin

Creative and reaching far beyond what others (and maybe you) believe can happen

Watch events carefully, act when the time is right, and soon what you want can be yours. Dare to be different. If seen in the bottom of the cup, it means you should avoid abandoning your dream; anything is possible. If seen in the middle of the cup, it shows you need to pay attention to what is truly obtainable and what is not—then go for it. If it appears on the rim, it shows that you are slowly rising to greater heights, like a giant airship. You will obtain your goals creatively.

Zodiac

*Any Sun sign symbol of the Zodiac
is a forewarning that there is an influence
from someone of that sign*

You may have a meeting with someone who has the Sun
sign image that appears. I once did a reading for a man
who had the symbol of Virgo in his cup. That evening
he met and later married someone with the Sun sign of
Virgo. If a symbol of the Zodiac appears in the bottom
of the cup, look for an old friend or someone who you
always wished you could meet. If seen in the middle of
the cup, it shows you will have an extremely important
business meeting soon, and a person with that sign will
be prominent. If it appears on the rim of the cup, it
shows you are about to meet a very interesting stranger,
with that sign, naturally.

5

SAMPLE READINGS

The sample readings on the following pages were taped and transcribed to give you an idea of how a real reading might progress. Your readings will probably follow a similar pattern, but each cup will present a different configuration of grounds. As you work with the grounds, your ability to *see* and interpret the symbols will grow, and before long you'll be reading for others.

Reading for Yourself

It is really easy to read the grounds. The best way to get started is to read your own grounds in your cup. I read my grounds every morning, or I read my husband's on a weekend morning, to see how his week will be. There is no right or wrong number of times a week someone can peer into the future. I make myself a cup of coffee every morning. I like mine black, but my husband likes his with milk and sugar—either is okay to use. I drink my coffee, and if I have a particular question I would like to know the answer to, then I think about my question. If I do not have a question, then I just enjoy my coffee. When I am just about finished, I add a pinch of grounds to the coffee that is left, and focus as I explained in the first part of this book. I do not drink all of the coffee, then I swish the grounds around in the cup and turn the cup, then holding the cup on its side and slowly turning the cup around counterclockwise three times. I make a wish or just slowly pour the liquid out onto the saucer. What remains are the grounds inside of the cup. Some may be on the bottom, or middle, or even the rim.

They represent the three phases of time: the past, present, and future. What I look for now is images. It is like looking at an abstract painting or clouds in the sky, I always ask myself: "What do you see?" Here is an example from a tape of a reading I gave myself recently:

"In the bottom of the cup I see the letter 'A,' and it is close to a picture of an airplane. Now I remember that letters of the alphabet are people. I have a good friend named Ann—we have known each other since childhood, but we have not seen each other lately.

"The airplane would indicate distance, which would make sense since she moved away last year. If I wanted to sound psychic and was giving someone else a reading, and I saw the same images in their cup, I would say: 'I see an A in your cup and an airplane—you must have a friend whom you miss who lives far away.' I already know that I miss my friend. I realize that I should contact her and tell her that she was in my cup.

"The next symbol I see, a jar, is in the middle of the cup. This reflects what is going on in my world right now. I have a major neighborhood project underway— the school is building a mural that my young son is involved with and I agreed to volunteer with this project. If I was giving a reading to another, I would tell them that they must be extremely busy with a major project, but to enjoy the work, for it would not last forever.

"On the rim of the cup is the future. I have a ball of yarn on the rim, which is saying that I am working like crazy on a project that will have far-reaching effects on others."

To me that sounds good, I like that—and so, in about five minutes, I have given myself an accurate reading. I would suggest if you want to read coffee grounds, sit back, have a cup of coffee, transport yourself to another time and place, and see what the grounds have in store for you.

Reading for Rusty

This is a coffee ground reading for Rusty, a single woman in her thirties, living in downtown Seattle. She is troubled and wants to know what is in her future.

Sophia: "OK, let's look in your cup. You seem very focused and that is good. I see lots of clear images."

Rusty: "Yes, I'm really concentrating. This is exciting."

S: "See this? An angel here on the rim of your cup brings you good news, especially with this dollar sign near it. This indicates that you will soon get a promotion or some sudden wealth. Oh, and let's see what else is here. When you see little clumps of grounds like this around the top of the cup, that involves money issues that are important now. Looking at this, it can mean that you spend money as fast as you make it, that you literally just toss it around. Since the grounds are touching the angel's foot, this means that due to a promotion or a raise or some sudden gift of money, you will have to spend some of your money on yourself for things like new clothes, make-up, that sort of thing. It really is a new image that you are after and that you will be projecting."

R: "Well, it looks like I'll soon get a new position in my company where I'll have to deal more with the public."

S: "Great. This is excellent for sales, communications, and the type of work that puts you in the public eye. This is really good. Now, over on the opposite side, I see a ring. Marriage is in the picture or being discussed, but because the ring is not perfectly round, you are having second thoughts. With this big heart over it, though, I would not be so worried. It definitely indicates love that is here to stay."

R: "That is absolutely true. I won't set a date, but maybe I should."

S: "Looking at the bottom of the cup, I can glimpse an image from your past and tell you that you lived in another state. It looks like California to me. Can you see the state image? Above the state is a bird. Birds are for the traveler, this shows the traveling and that you love to be on the go."

R: "My company is based in Sacramento and they just transferred me here!"

S: "This house-like image shows that you also have a desire to own your own home. Next to the house is a question mark—are you going to buy that dream home? Just thinking about it? Or are you going to wait?"

Reading with Bill

This is a reading with Bill. He is a very successful writer and journalist, and he wants a birthday reading to see how the coming year will be.

Bill: "So, now what do I do? I now have my coffee."

Sophia: "Yes, I would like you to drink your coffee and drink as much as you like. You do not have to drink all of it. I just need to have a little essence of you in the cup, so drink as much as you like."

B: "Do I have to think of anything special? Do I ask special questions or what?"

S: "Yes, If there is an area of something that you are extremely interested in like money, then that is what you would concentrate on. It is possible, though, just to have an open mind and see how things will go."

B: "Well, I am just going to be open to see how things will go. Today is my birthday, and I want to see what kind of year it will be."

S: "Birthday readings are great to see how the year is going to be, so you may want to think about what your year might be like."

B: "All right, I will think about what my year might be. That sounds good."

S: "For myself, I do it every day to see what my day would be like, but certainly you can do it any way that you want."

B: "Okay, I am done with my coffee."

S: "Oh, you are done with your coffee. Good."

B: "What are you doing now?"

S: "I am adding grounds to your coffee. I learned to read the grounds when percolators were popular. With percolators there were always grounds left in the cup. Now, with new types of coffeemakers there really are not any grounds left in the cup so you have to add some, which is just fine. What I also need to tell you is that it is best to add the grounds after you drink your coffee. You really do not want to drink the grounds."

B: "What am I supposed to do now?"

S: "You pour out the remains of your coffee, turning the cup counterclockwise three times as you pour, thinking the whole time what you want to have resolved in the grounds."

B: "So I pour the remaining coffee out in my saucer?"

S: "Yes, pour it out counterclockwise three times."

B: "Okay. I am ready."

S: "Interesting. When you look in someone's cup, you are looking for patterns, telltale numbers, or letters. Grounds in the bottom of the cup show the past, the middle of the cup the present, and the rim of the cup the future. Looking in the bottom of the cup, there really are not any grounds. No grounds in the bottom indicates that you are a person who does not worry about what might have been, or could have been. A lot of grounds in the middle and on the rim of the cup is a person who is concerned about the here and now. Also the future is something you think a lot about."

B: "That is true."

S: "Now, you said you wanted a reading for a year, a birthday reading."

B: "I'd like one for now and for the future."

S: "I am seeing some interesting patterns. Let me move into the light. It is best to use a cup that is white inside, so you can see the grounds. If the inside of the cup is dark, then it is impossible to see the grounds. The first picture that I see is a windmill. You are trying to find the pace in life that will help you succeed—not moving so fast, not moving too slow. But you feel like you're not really getting anywhere. You also have a an image of a guitar. You are a musical person and may have artistic talent. Do you play an instrument or do you have an interest in music?"

B: "This is interesting, because I just got a letter from a music producer who likes my book and would like to collaborate with me, to make an album. I recorded a lot of music from my travels and he thought of mixing them into some song. It is something I do not feel that I am capable of, but maybe I am."

S: "This is interesting because the guitar in your cup is off to the side. It is as if this is something that came out of the blue, that you were not expecting."

B: "Very true, it took me completely by surprise."

S: "A sun is in your cup—which is a wonderful symbol—you are a person with an outgoing, sunny personality. People like you, and you like people. You also have two people holding hands in your cup. A partnership is important to you and you feel grounded when you are with another. Also in your cup is a symbol of Scorpio, which is not very psychic of me to say you must be a Scorpio, since you already told me it is your birthday, really it is pretty obvious."

B: (Laughs) "Well, I could have been a Libra."

S: "When you look at grounds you do not want to say 'oh, I see a bunch of grounds in my cup.' Look at the grounds in a more abstract way, like at a modern art painting, formation of clouds, or as glyphs that you would see at a famous archaeological site."

B: "Kind of like letting your eyes go out of focus?"

S: "Right, like looking at those 3D pictures in the mall. You know, I never see the image in 3D pictures. Coffee grounds are much easier. Let me look back at your cup—you are a person who needs a lot of courage in the near future. You have the face of a lion in your cup, so you must be brave, put on the fierce proud look of the lion. These are attributes of your personality that are already there, but now you are going to have to use them. You also have a star in your cup, so you have a lot of personal power right now—you are a star. So this is the time to decide who you want to be. What do you want to be known for? What do you want to accomplish?"

B: "I want my book to be published."

S: "Let me see if that is possible. You have an anchor in your cup, which indicates that you bring your anchor down. What do you think an anchor means?"

B: "Stability."

S: "Right, and the anchor is on the rim so it is stability in the future. See, you can read the grounds on your own—you do not need me. It's your money, though, so give me a hundred bucks for the reading."

B & S: (Laugh)

S: "You have a big "K" in your cup. This person will become extremely important this year."

B: "That's my agent; her last name starts with "K."

S: "She is a person who strongly identifies with who she is, and uses her last name a lot. Let me look around your cup and see if I am getting any more images. No, it looks like a pretty good year for you. The stability you desire will come to you. Your agent will come through for you this year. The sun and lion are very strong character attributes that you will soon be using. The windmill is telling you to be steady and soon things will change, and the guitar is a twist of fate. The outcome will be favorable and surprise you. Last is the anchor, which is really well formed—a long-time desire will come true. Dream and do your dreams, life is about to offer you many happy things. Happy Birthday, Bill. Do you have any questions?"

B: "No, that was great. Thank you very much."